THE KITCHEN HEALER

THE KITCHEN HEALER

the journey to becoming you

jules blaine davis

sounds true
BOULDER, COLORADO

Sounds True
Boulder, CO 80306

Published 2022

Cover and book design by Linsey Dodaro
Cover photo by Molly Donna Ware

Pages x, 3, 4, 6–7, 16, 30–31, 32, 36, 42, 48, 50, 57, 58, 60, 72, 77, 78, 83, 87, 92, 98–99,
100, 104, 118, 132–133, 137, 157, 158, 168, 174, 180, 184, 186, 190, 206, 212, 221, 234, 239,
250–251, 256–257, 262, 266, 268: Photos © Miranda Hayek—Blossom Blue Studio.

Pages iii, viii, 10, 12, 14, 19 (upper), 35, 40, 91, 97, 108, 114, 116, 130–131, 134, 140, 143,
147, 222, 225, 227, 230, 255, 258: Photos © Molly Donna Ware.

Pages v, vii, 19 (lower), 20, 22, 39, 47, 75, 80, 84, 103, 110, 123, 124, 127, 128, 153, 161,
162, 165, 177, 179, 183, 195, 196, 198, 201, 202, 219, 229, 240, 242, 252–253: Photos ©
Jules Blaine Davis.

Page 66: Photo © Cynthia Perez.
Page 275: Author photo © Joe Pugliese.

Pages 6–7: Wooden dolls by Elizabeth Rainer.
Page 42: Drawing by Beauty Cleopatra Fischer.
Page 57: Painting by Jules Blaine Davis.
Page 77: Painting by Jennifer Mercede.
Page 153: Poem by Jacqueline Suskin.
Page 266: Artwork by Linda Oldham.

Printed in Canada

BK06390

Library of Congress Cataloging-in-Publication Data
Names: Davis, Jules Blaine, author.
Title: The kitchen healer : the journey to becoming you / Jules Blaine Davis.
Description: Boulder, CO : Sounds True, [2022] | Includes bibliographical
references.
Identifiers: LCCN 2021059806 (print) | LCCN 2021059807 (ebook) | ISBN
9781683649205 (hardcover) | ISBN 9781683649212 (ebook)
Subjects: LCSH: Healing--Religious aspects. | Self-realization in women. | Spiritual
life. | Cooking--Religious aspects. | Cooking--Psychological aspects.
Classification: LCC BL65.M4 D345 2022 (print) | LCC BL65.M4 (ebook) | DDC
203/.1--dc23/eng20220521
LC record available at https://lccn.loc.gov/2021059806
LC ebook record available at https://lccn.loc.gov/2021059807

10 9 8 7 6 5 4 3 2 1

for Her
for all of our mothers
everywhere

to ocean & beauty

may you always become you
love you x x x x
mama

Courage, my love
you are enough

Courage, my love
you are everything

contents

permission everywhere

The door is open, and you are right on time. As you walk up to the front porch, you see a pair of biggish black Vans, smallish rainbow boots, high-top garden galoshes, and fuchsia sneakers near a tattered doormat that says "You are gorgeous." As you lift your gaze to the windowsill, you see rocks and shells, a few ceramic hearts, and the word "LOVE" painted in hot pink on a piece of driftwood. You can take your shoes off here, drop your bags, and let go of anything that might be in the way of you being here. As you look through the screen door, you see a lit beeswax candle on the dining room table with a heart-shaped wood board next to it. You hear music— Rising Appalachia, Alicia Keys, or Chaka Khan, depending on the mood. As you make your way inside, you feel a warmth of goodness and love that brings you closer to the kitchen. On your way, you see the heart-shaped wood board with sliced Gala apples, white nectarines, some goat gouda, rice crackers, and a small bowl of Castelvetrano olives.

This is for you.

Everywhere you look, you see a kind of *messy beauty* inside day-to-day things, like a wide wood bowl holding a soft mountain of unfolded linen and cotton napkins, or a cracked cake plate offering the season's bounty. Fuyu persimmons, Gold Nugget tangerines, and a heart-shaped rock with the word "courage" painted on it. These are daily moments made sacred by the way they are offered inside the flow of a freely creative aesthetic. There is nothing to hide here. This is permission everywhere. Permission to feel all your senses, to take everything in and receive the ease and freedom that is here. The aroma of a cake, light and rising, guides you gently into the kitchen. This is where you will find me, steeping our love tea, opening a wide vat of golden sage honey to stir inside our time together.

I see you, and I am so happy you are here.

The cabinet is open for you to choose from a variety of porcelain teacups, ceramic mugs, and handmade clay vessels. They are close together, a few nestled one inside the other, yet each one has its own feeling. Choose a vessel that feels like home in the palms of your hands. You can take your time here. As you turn around, you will see a wall of wood boards, open salt bowls, a block of butter on a round blue plate next to three eggs nuzzled together in a little pink pinch pot by the stove. There is a freedom that comes with placing the ingredients you use daily out in the open. When you can see, feel, and be with what you love, you become more connected to yourself. This is not clutter. It is intentional and has the essence of YOU embodied everywhere. This daily invitation to acknowledge, honor, and remember what you love awakens everything. Permission everywhere not only supports your healing, it makes space for you to embody possibilities you couldn't see—until now.

There is nothing to do.

There is nothing to fix.

There is no rush.

This is for YOU.

This book, like my kitchen, is a soft place to land. It is also base camp for the journey ahead. We will return to the kitchen again and again as you make your way toward yourself. In the warmth of the kitchen, you might feel an opening or an unraveling toward a spaciousness within you. This might bring up a longing or a yearning for something you can't yet name. With the tinctures of permission, freedom, and beauty, you might begin to feel a hunger not only for a piece of olive oil cake, but for this deeper sense of yourself. You might not even know that you are hungry. That's okay—many of us have no idea how hungry we truly are. We run in circles around our lives and call it a living. We book our days over-full, with *the right thing to do* or *what needs to get done.* This is how we have been conditioned to live. You have no time for yourself, so you go missing inside your own life. You keep giving, going, and doing, trying to stay safe and save others from their pain. You repeat the words "I know" when someone tells you that you need to take a break, but your actions say, "I will get to me later." You are so busy carrying these old stories from your childhood, your lineage, and your culture that you forgot you have a self, a body, a story to write, a life to live, and a legacy to become.

> You ask others what they are hungry for, maybe you forgot to ask yourself: What are YOU hungry for?

You are hungry for the love inside permission and beauty and freedom. You are hungry for the lightness inside ease, flow, and authentic connection. You are hungry for Mother Earth and the intimate relationship waiting for you inside a wood board love and a carrot-ginger soup simmering on the back burner. Even if you don't like ginger, all of a sudden, you are hungry for it. You are hungry to be seen and heard and felt. You are hungry to know who you are, beneath the errands and the busyness and all the doing.

You are hungry to become YOU.

As you feel the unconditional love flowing through the kitchen, a new way of *doing and being* will emerge. Curiosity and willingness lead the way to the creativity and truth of your living. We are going to find permission everywhere as we move through this journey together. We will find it in the pantry, in the cabinets, and on the kitchen counters. We will feel it in the rhythm, cadence, and flow of your days and nights. We will discover your values and leave behind the stories that are in the way to you claiming the life you long to live. We will go at your pace with a love nudge

from me. I will meet you where you are. I will offer recipes from *the loving you trade.* You can start right now. Ask yourself: *Am I loving my day?* You can check in to see if what you are *doing* is an act of loving for you and your body. I can hear you . . . the bills, the marriage, the work, what will they think, what will I think, and so on. I got you. We are here together. And this is your journey to embark on.

This journey is a devotion quest. *You* are your beloved. And when permission and beauty surround you, they offer the limitless gift of becoming you. You begin to embody your becoming. This is custom, intimate, and powerful. Your healing is not superficial, nor is it something topical to float on the surface of your life.

You will wake up, turn on the fire, find your body, cook up a feast with ease—becoming who you are, again and again. Who knew that the aroma of a cake permeating through the house, a circle of women around a fire, and the feeling of your feet rooted to the ground at the kitchen island could feed you in such deep ways. And this is just the beginning to meeting your hunger and nourishing your becoming.

nourishing my life

My path to nourishing—myself and the world around me—broke ground on many Wednesdays around 5:30 a.m. We had one car, a black VW Jetta station wagon. I would take the car seats out, put the seats down, and throw the stroller in along with three or four baskets; a few canvas bags; empty berry, cherry, tomato, and egg cartons; cardboard flats; and one big, black crate. I would drive across the city, from the east to the west as the sun rose to light my way. No matter how tired I was, I didn't miss a market.

As I got closer to 4th Street, I would feel a familiar excitement inside me. What would I find? What had grown since last week? What farms would be there? With breastfeeding pads in my bra, an apron tied around my waist, and money for overdue bills in my pocket, I was ready.

I was usually one of the first to arrive. It was me and my grayish silver Graco stroller waiting for the barricades to move aside. The only other people who arrived this early were the chefs in their white coats and black clogs, mostly, if not all, male, hauling their crate-filled

dollies from vendor to vendor. They seemed to have an incredibly important purpose. I was ravenous and a bit of a mystery. We were the early birds, like crows wandering the streets at dawn, scanning tables for whatever was ripe and ready.

They were curious about me—who did I work for and what was I going to do with *all that food?* I was curious about me, too. Most of the women with strollers showed up with actual kids in them, at a time that made sense, with a balloon tied to the stroller handle and a French baguette protruding from the bottom basket. My stroller carried my kids most days, but on Wednesday mornings, she was *my dolly.* She wasn't one of the fancy ones, but she was relentless in how she carried me and all that I was gathering inside this time.

gathering beauty

I filled her to the brim with thick-stemmed artichokes, bunches of watermelon radishes, Japanese turnips, red kuri squashes, Nantes carrots, Salanova lettuces, chocolate

Hayicha persimmons, red walnuts, Persian mulberries, and all the seasonal goodness I could find. All the variety and abundance was a miracle! The colors of the season stopped me in my tracks. The taste of tended soil inside the first spring asparagus, or a bunch of green garlic with that skinny violet stripe rounding the peel, was a radical kind of intimacy. I didn't know how to cook most of what I gathered; I just knew I needed to bring it all home. Beauty was writing me a love note, inviting me closer to myself. It felt like freedom was undoing me in the best way. I was learning a new language inside those bright fuchsia figs from Italy with the celadon striped skin. They looked like a haute couture silk circus tent made for an Hermès spring collection in the 80s.

I was falling in love.

I had entered a beautiful world where I could nourish my family, heal my body, feed the community, and so much more! This world of beauty was doing more than feeding me: it was restoring, resuscitating, and recovering parts of me that had been suppressed by the old stories I was carrying. Stories written by a cultureless culture, a hungry lineage, and a family of origin that modeled separating from our true selves in order to survive and belong. I was forever in a rush and very late to a life *I should be living*. The *I can do it all* mindset kept me from myself for many years. I was tired, stressed, and scared. I was also joyous, grateful, and deeply rooted to mothering my family. I had a fire inside me to change the patterns from which I came. All I "needed" (old story) was to find "success" (particularly with money) and prove to "everyone" (whoever that was) that I was capable of something amazing.

In other words: I would *do things*, be seen and praised for *doing things*, and get to the deep stuff later. I was the deep stuff. Borrrring story alert: this is one of many borrrring stories so many of us carry around in our bodies until we let go (which can feel scary) and let something deeper in (which might feel scarier), allowing us to live lighter inside our lives, which is the most phenomenal feeling ever.

Walking, gathering, being at the market became my healing. It carried me across thresholds of early

motherhood, marriage, and a recession, just to name a few. The beauty I found there reminded me that I am everything. I am the crows, I am the stroller, I am the farmer, I am the figs, I am the earth, I am possibility. Discovering this was the awakening that brought me closer to myself and nourished the artist in me. To gather beauty and create food to feed me and my family became foundational to who I am. *Wait, who am I again?* That was the question! I had forgotten that I was a performer, a dancer, a singer, a painter, a poet. While I was loving my babies and doing what I needed to do as a wife and mother, I had forgotten all the other parts of me that I loved.

We forget ourselves when we go hungry inside our lives. Often, we don't even know we are hungry. We don't even know we have a self. Yet, what I didn't see—in the culture or in my lineage or at the preschool parking lot—was a mother nourishing herself as she nourished her family. I had not seen this . . . YET.

finding myself in the kitchen

Bringing this beauty home felt like a party without the "it's an event" stress. When I laid everything out on the kitchen table, it was like a scene in *Mary Poppins*—a few blue jays with their little beaks opening the cabinets, and monarch butterflies sliding drawers open with their wings, fluttering with joy. You could find me whistling as more little yellow, orange, and navy-blue birdies gathered wood bowls, cake plates, and a few heirloom dishes, holding them in the air next to my pink hair. We would look at each other lovingly, with sparkly glitter in our eyes.

I filled bowls with Seascape strawberries, Hass avocadoes, Kishu tangerines, mango nectarines, Red Delicious apples, and all that the season had to offer that week. I created sacred spaces on the table, in the corners, and on the counters. I was creating altars with food— even in the fridge. I turned on Patty Griffin, India Arie, or Angélique Kidjo, depending on the mood. I felt my feet on the floor as I grabbed a wood board and a bread knife. I cut figs in half, sliced a ripe Bartlett pear, poured out some blueberries, and added a few thin slices of smoked salmon. My two-year-old son, Ocean, would look up at me, holding onto my calf and smiling, as I set our wood board love on his little table. We would dance and eat and laugh as I cooked up what I had gathered at the market. (We are still doing this today! Now he cooks too!) I found myself steaming golden beets with the peel on, discovering that the hard, protective skin slides off when it's warm and softened. I was becoming warm and softened as I steeped milky love tea and found my way inside a Tuscan bean soup simmering on low, creating an aroma that made our house a home. I was getting closer to myself, my family, and the earth. I was learning how to nourish myself as I nourished them.

a deeper hunger

It would be a minute—or fifteen years— before I began to write down what was cooking up inside of me. At the time, I started a blog as evidence that I was alive and doing *something*. This was the

beginning of the era of blogs, so I thought, *Why not?* (And yes, this was before Instagram—can you imagine?) It didn't make me famous or land me a book deal. It was a place where I could be alone for four seconds and jot down a few field notes between nap times and what I might be roasting. As I was cooking up this way of living, my friend Ana, a birth doula and mother, invited me to feed the women who attended her birth classes and the events she offered to the community. This felt aligned with how I was rebirthing myself inside the kitchen. I said YES.

It was not a catering job. I was feeding women during a threshold time, a time of their becoming. And I was feeding myself inside a threshold time, a time of *my* becoming! I gathered seasonal goodness at the market just like I did for my family. I gathered with love and possibility and permission. These women could feel this love in the food. They would ask how I cooked the red lentils or what I put on the roasted carrots to *make them so sweet.* I told them about the market and how gathering food in this way was healing something deep inside of me. I asked how they were cooking—in the kitchen and in their lives. This opened up stories about their mothers and grandmothers, about the kitchens of their childhoods, about how they woke up in the morning all the way to this moment we are in right now. They expressed how far away they felt from themselves. They would say, "I don't even know who I am anymore!" as they took another bite of warm, loving food. Hugging me goodbye, they shared that, just sitting together like this, they felt closer to themselves than they had in years, if ever. They asked me what they could do to feel like this in their own lives. The question I was hearing under their question was, *How can I remember who I am?*

Listening to these women and receiving their experiences inspired me in a deep way. Being hungry for yourself and not knowing it is a silent epidemic—silent because no one talks about it. I was discovering that to nourish yourself inside a busy life is to rewrite the conditioned narrative you (we) carry in your (our) body. I realized that *being* in the kitchen is a healing *inside our lives*. It is deeply courageous work to heal inside a cultureless culture that is ravenous for itself. This kind of work requires taking a journey.

At this time, living a more organic lifestyle was becoming popular in the US. Pioneers like Alice Waters and Michael Pollan were at the forefront, shining light on ways of eating that aligned with the earth. A few years later, words like "shame" and "grief" would start trending thanks to the powerful work of Brené Brown. Her research on courage and vulnerability validated the emotional landscapes we walk through inside our everyday lives. These words and how they were beginning to weave through the mainstream supported the heartfelt language I was cooking up inside of me. Now when I said the words "grief" or "shame" in conversations with women I would meet at the market, they wouldn't all run away from me. A few would actually get a little closer and want to know more.

This conversation about hunger and longing was deep and wide, honest and true. It wasn't solely about food (and yet everything is about food). Books about the journeys we take to become who we are were on the rise thanks to brave writers like Elizabeth Gilbert, Glennon Doyle, and Cheryl Strayed. They were leaving their day-to-day lives to venture far and wide, following a calling to sate something deeper. They were naming the pain that separated them from themselves and voicing it for all of us to hear.

The story I was cooking up was something I hadn't seen yet. I was on my own kind of vision quest, standing at the kitchen counter, pulsing the Cuisinart to transform something inside me. I was as hungry as those writers, yet I had to breastfeed before the nap, put the wet clothes into the dryer, and roast a chicken within forty-five minutes. *My trip around the world* was running out the door with a baby on one hip, to get to preschool pickup, soccer practice, while passing my painting studio on my way to grab the keys to the car. It was in returning to the kitchen again and again, where I could meet myself, feel my body, sing and cry as I made dinner, a soup for a friend, and a crumble for tomorrow's breakfast. I was learning how to heal *inside* my life.

showing the way

In time, I invited a few women to meet me at the market. I asked them to bring baskets, bags, a stroller or a cart, walking shoes, cash, and a hat for the sun. I requested that they come on their own—no babies, kids, or partners; just themselves. This was the beginning of their healing. Asking them to come on their own was like saying, "Let's take a month and go to Morocco." Guiding them through *the language of asking for support* from their partners or caregivers was like asking them to jump out of a plane with no parachute. *Leave ample space for yourself before and after our time together, prepare the car the night before, make sure you have gas in the tank and a water bottle ready to go* were just a few ideas I offered to make this easeful and doable for them. I was asking them to take care of themselves—something new for them, though they took care of everyone else. Another borrrring story alert. I was so hungry for us to rewrite these boring and conditional stories together.

They met me at 7:45 a.m. on a Sunday morning, in the center of the Hollywood Farmers' Market. Our first stop was Dave's Korean Food, where we gathered warm broth to sip as we began our journey. Drinking this warmth helped us center ourselves, inviting us to slow down from our usual rushed, getting-it-done energy, to feel our bodies and move through the busy market from a more grounded place. Just this was healing. Moving slower with intention, we got the job done in a very efficient yet peaceful way—we could be in our bodies and do the delicious work of gathering our food and learning how to cook it. We could be full and light *inside* the doing.

I introduced them to the farmers and the kind people running the stands. Building these relationships was a wonderful part of gathering in this way. I was drawn to the farmers with love in their eyes, goodness in their hands and soil stains on their skin. They usually had something exciting to teach or share with me. You could feel how they cared for the food and their love for how we were all growing together inside this time. I encouraged the women to seek this feeling out when they were drawn to a certain table, to listen for what felt good to them. I was inviting us to trust this voice inside, to let our intuition—this felt sense of our heart's wisdom—guide us. It was also good to ask if something was organic or how it was grown, where the farm was located, and how long the soil had been tended in this loving way. Using their voices to ask about their food and get curious about what they were putting in their body created connection and a level of care for themselves that was new and vital.

We tasted a variety of fruits and veggies of the season; I taught them where and how to store each one once they got home. I shared what to get cooking as they brought this beauty into the kitchen and to their family. My recipes included timing and temperature—but cooking was the easy part. I was more focused on how the women were going to *get into the kitchen*, to cross the threshold into this space of being with their whole selves with all the other needs of family, work, and life. I was inviting them to bring their body with them as they turned on the fire and found ways to move, stretch, and breathe. I encouraged them to begin dinner in the morning, getting that aroma going so it could hold whatever the day brought in.

I offered ideas like cutting the cauliflower with scissors, using a pie plate for roasting small root vegetables like turnips and radishes, using cake plates for holding berries, and letting go of serving things hot and perfect and other fancy chef ideas that were left over from old, archived (borrrring) stories. My offerings were not just about food and cooking; they were about creating ritual and intention inside the life you want to live. My recipes were about permission everywhere. In approaching food this way, the women were connecting with something deeper within themselves, so they could nourish themselves and others from a full place. All of a sudden, the overwhelm or anxiety they might have felt before moved into a sacred place of healing. This way of healing was a way of living. And this way of living was lighting the way to what their day-to-day life could feel like when tended from the heart of the kitchen instead of the frantic, busy chaos that left them staring into an empty fridge asking, "What's for dinner?"

a miracle

Now that these women were gathering food at the market and had a few recipes to prepare, I invited them into my kitchen, which was more like a hallway between two countertops. One might call it "modern." I began by moving the rectangular dining table next to the oven, as we needed to be as close to the fire as possible. The table overflowed with cake plates of yellow, red, and zebra-striped heirloom tomatoes; wood boards with sliced Honeycrisp apples and green pluots; goat brie oozing with thin ribbons of honey on top; sliced yellow peaches; buffalo mozzarella; and steamed artichokes alongside wide, empty bowls for the leaves. As I gathered and created this beauty, I would hear poems that wanted to be read, stories that needed to be told, music that wanted to be played. It was like a hip-hop symphony of inspired amazingness moving through my body. I was like a rabbi-DJ-midwife being guided by something much bigger than me.

As word spread about these kitchen lovefests, six or eight women would gather in my kitchen on a weekday to experience what I called *a miracle*. As they came in, I poured milky Mauritius tea in their cups, inviting them to lean into this moment right here. They came from a variety of backgrounds, religions, and ethnicities. They were new or soon-to-be moms, empty nesters, grandmothers, newlyweds, step-moms new to mothering, and single women learning how to mother their lives. They all had one thing in common: they were hungry to be fed. Many would share that they had heard about this through a friend, and they had no idea what was going to happen. "Me too," I would say. Our laughter brought lightness into the unknown as the women received the abundance of the table, feeling the warmth of the tea mug in their hands. I invited us to slow it wayyyyy down, to close our eyes and connect with our breath. I was creating something I had never seen before—a space of unconditional loving to nourish ourselves fully. A place to be held, seen, and heard. A place to become who we are as we let go of the old stories we thought we needed to carry around. We were crossing a threshold into a powerful conversation that would continue to change our lives forever.

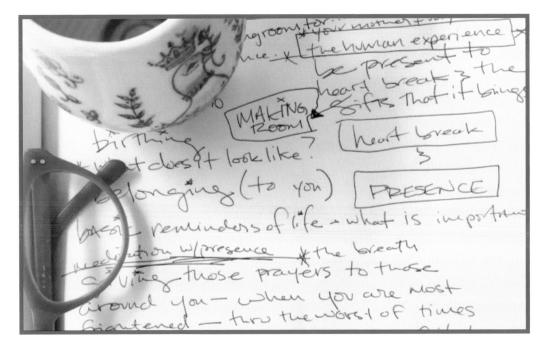

me too medicine

The freedom to turn on the fire, in the kitchen and in your life, is one and the same. Food, tea, and women. Laughter, tears, and poems. Oh the stories we were rewriting! Sitting together around the table with women who carved out this time for themselves and the fire on, nourishing our wholeness with food and poetry, felt like the best way to heal. It still is. As the women were settling in, nourishing their hearts and bodies, they began to share their stories and all the ways they had been shaped. There were stories about motherless daughters, latchkey kids, divorce, sexual and physical abuse, and survival, as the butternut squash softened in the pot with salted butter and peeled apples for our soup. In between the stories, someone would ask if the skin on the fig was edible. Another would mention how incredible the radish with the goat cheese and honey was and how everyone had to try it. This is what we do when we are being nourished: we fill ourselves up to share and feed each other.

I would make another batch of tea, pour a good amount of raw cream, and stir the warm Ball jar with a wood spoon like a magic cauldron. Round and round, like these women's stories, spinning gold as they were held by the limitless love we were creating together. We were healing as a collective. Each woman being transformed by the others' stories, and the *me too medicine* lightening the heaviness each woman had carried into this miracle. In sharing our stories, we were becoming one whole, holy, rewritten story. I was showing them how to cook and heal and live and grow while *doing their lives* and *being in their lives* at the same time. They were learning how to get ahead of the busyness and build a new foundation—one where they are nourished from a full place. This is where limitless possibility lives. There were no sacrifices to make or selves to leave behind. I moved around the kitchen with ease and delight, elated to share what was supporting me to rewrite my own story.

I turned on the oven to 375 degrees as I gathered a casserole dish, olive oil, and an open bowl of salt. I placed the unpeeled carrots in the dish, and a few parsnips too. I twisted the tops until they released their hold, placing them in the open bowl beside me. I poured the olive oil with freedom in my wrist, added salt, and massaged everything with my hands. The veil of a million excuses about *how hard* or *no time* or *not for me* dissolved before their eyes. Hope, excitement, and a newfound energy rose with the aroma of the root vegetables softening in the oven. I shared about the love we put in our food, and how when we bring our pain, suffering, grief, fear, and joy to this love, we heal. We become our own healer.

I was becoming a kitchen healer.

YES.

The path of healing begins with the word YES. I am offering you my resounding YES. My yes for you is inside every page of this book. Your journey to your yes begins with an openness to loving yourself. This can feel like very intimate terrain because it is.

You might ask, *Why is it important to nourish my life?* Another way to say this is, *Why do I need to know who I am?* Many of us don't know who we really are. We live our lives from the outside in. We support others, we meet needs, we react to the outside first, and rarely, if ever, do we get around to ourselves. Whether or not you're aware of it, your life is shaped by the decisions you make. This is where the invitation to this journey begins. There is a world inside of you. It is vast and lush and full of gorgeous offerings just for YOU.

This book is like a compass for your interior as you navigate the terrain inside of you. Venturing within connects you deeply to who you are. And it is a forever conversation. To carry an inner compass in the landscape of a famished culture is the journey of a pioneer. And here you thought you would just gather a few soup recipes and call it a day! Please go ahead and flip through the pages to see what you might want to have cooking while you make your way inside. No matter what, I am right beside you.

what will you find inside?

In just a few pages, you will find your permission slip. You must sign this before you go on. Just kidding! You can do whatever you feel called to do, which is the entire point of permission and the invitation to remember WHO YOU ARE! How you experience permission and freedom is essential here. Many of us seek out the opposite of how we were raised and shaped. If you were brought up in a more conservative or strict home, you might be *free* in a way that doesn't have any boundaries, accountability, or groundedness, which might leave you lost in your days, reactive and trying to find your purpose. If it was *loosey goosey* in your home of origin, you might find that you are quite organized, even overly disciplined, which doesn't leave room or space for who you might want to become.

That is why this is journey work. You are going on a journey to the middle way, the place that feels most aligned to who you are. *Who are you?* We're going to find out! Leaving the butter out on a plate you love, or seeing an altar of words or clay or wood totems as you wash the dishes supports you in making your way toward YOU. As you remember you, you make room for the medicine permission brings, which can deeply nourish your life. Permission isn't a luxury here. It is an essential ingredient to becoming you. At any moment you can slow it down and check in with yourself. I have set up lots of places for you to do this along the way. This book is divided into four parts or ingredients in the recipe to becoming you, plus lots of resources and kitchen healer love in the appendix. This is *your* journey. You are at the wheel. I am in the passenger seat with a flashlight, our field guide, a few custom-made maps, some really wonderful tinctures and tools, like worn wood spoons, soft linens, and a few poems to help us along.

In part one, "Waking Up: The Stories We Carry," I ask you the question, *How did you wake up?* In the morning, as a child in your home of origin. You will spend some time here with this question. You might sit beside it, make it a love tea and unpack what is here for you. In time, you will bring the inquiry with you into this moment right here: *How are you waking up in your life today?* In the morning, in the day, at your job, in your marriage, wherever you want to go with it. As you show up to this question, you might feel something (or you might feel nothing for a minute before you feel something). This something might feel like grief or loss or sadness or heaviness awakening inside. This is where the gold lives. You might begin to see a connection, a repeating rhythm or pattern, or an intuitive song you have always heard but never made time to listen to . . . until now. These voices and emotional wisdoms are waiting to be woven into your rewritten story. All you have to do is show up. Everything is here for you.

I will invite you to feel your feelings and bring all that you are recovering to the fire as you make your way to part two, "Turning on the Fire: Haaaaaaaaa." This is where you and your stories will meet your breath (haaaaaaaaa), stretch your body, put on the kettle, make a tea, and soften into what has been here with you all along. You will learn about the medicine inside the mornings and how your breath can heal you. You will become an offering to the fire as you discover what it looks like to tend to the fire inside of you. As you show up and create a practice in the day-to-day, something inside of you will rise to the surface.

It is here that you realize you are really on this journey, no going back, and that no matter what you might think, you are indeed changing.

As you feel this transformation occurring, you move into "You Have a Body: The Middle Way." These pages are like no other in the book. You are on the bridge crossing over all that you are healing, heading toward an intimate reunion with your body. This is where you can mooooove and be moooooved with music you love and any feelings that have gotten stuck, immersed, or mired along the way. You can come back to The Middle Way at any point in your journey. You have a body! Your body is your home. Your body is your kitchen. Your body is everything, and you can move it whenever and however you like. And as you move what is stuck or hard or heavy, you make room for the wisdom that has been waiting to hold you. Everything you are waiting for is right here in your body. To write about moving the body, on a page like this, with words and paper, where you can't hear inspiring music or my voice, is its own impossible crayness . . . AND I did it anyway! It is

so vital for you to move what comes up in your everyday life, and then let it go. Your body is so incredible! Will you move with me? You will feel soooooo much lighter, I promise.

As you begin to feel lighter with your new, yet old, wisdom guiding the way, you can bring yourself into the kitchen for part three, "Healing in the Kitchen: Cooking Up a Life You Love." You must eat so you can nourish and feed your wisdom. So much goodness is happening in here with ease, freedom, and—yep, you guessed it—permission! You are so ready for what you are about to *do and be*. Everything you have gathered and laid out on the kitchen island has prepared you for this moment. You are going to heal in the kitchen with food and the fire and your body! You are going to create *a place to be* as you cook up the life you long for. You are showing up to a practice that nourishes you, creating a culture in your home called *wood board love*. This section of the book is beauty-FULL with recipes and remedies you can return to all the time.

As you feel your life changing in the kitchen, you will find yourself longing to bring it home in part four, "Becoming You: A Forever Conversation." You are gathering all that you have foraged and harvested. You are seeing and feeling and hearing your experiences. You are integrating what is true for you as you gather a team that can support you, inspire you, and reflect to you as you keep moving toward yourself. You are valuing you. You are healing as a way of living. You are inside of your forever conversation. As you dim the lights to the kitchen and begin to close it up for the night, you feel, maybe for the first time, how held you are. You are becoming you.

poetry

Throughout this book and your journey, you will find poetry offering its powerful medicine. These are moments for feeling your heart and receiving the wisdom that is making its way to you across every page. Poetry is an intimate place to sit and be deeply nourished. It is the most delicious snack. It can also reveal a view to a feeling inside that you have never seen or acknowledged before. Every time you read a poem, make sure to read it out loud so you can hear your own voice as you feel the words

land lovingly inside you. The poems in this book are placed intentionally as bridges into the next page or section. They will support you to take the next step into a deeper part of yourself.

words & their basic definitions

As you read, you will also come across key words with their basic definitions. Consider this a place to center and reorient yourself to your journey. Words make up the language we use to tell our stories and live our lives. We carry these words around and even claim them as our own, sometimes forgetting what they actually mean. They become a part of our cellular structure; this is why creating new language is essential in a healing journey. Detangling these words from the emotional DNA that originally informed your old stories can be painful, difficult, and even scary. Consider these places in the book to be a water fountain, refreshing and quenching your thirst for new ways of being. This is another invitation to slow down and reassess what you are saying to yourself and others. Oh, don't worry—it's not all about you. It's about *us*. When you heal your language, you change your mind. This change is for everyone. Everyone heals.

heart work & hello, body!

"Heart work" is homework for your heart. This is your workbook inviting you deeper into your journey. You can do heart work in the sequence that is offered here, or choose what feels good in the moment. Everything is here for YOU. "Hello, body!" is heart work for your body! It is a simple reminder to come back to your body. It is here to remind you that you have a body!

recipes

The recipes in this book are medicine ways for dinner, for life, for a sad day, for a party, for a birth . . . all the way to sitting shivah by the fire. They are seasonal blueprints for the year or the day. These recipes have been collected and kept over many years—from my childhood to early motherhood to now. They are on a seasonal rotation in my home, guiding my connection with the earth and my body. They have been the mothers, grandmothers, healers, and

elders I needed in the moment. May they find that special place in your kitchen, creating a legacy to nourish you, your family, and all those you love. May they inspire you to turn on the fire and remember who you are as you cook up a life you love.

cake wisdom

There is cake wisdom here, too! I didn't plan for this, yet it was just here, staring me in the face, like a soothsayer's mystery missive, waiting until I read the whole book for the first time to discover I placed a cake recipe at the end of each section. Maybe it was my hungry muse or perhaps Spirit coming through with Her higher wisdom for us. Here is the wisdom: at the end of the day or the section, no matter what happens in your incredible life, you can always bake a cake! And let's face it, cake is the ultimate healer. I don't mean *stuff your face and push down your pain* cake; I mean the cake you make for brekkie, lunch, dinner, and all the times in between. As you show up for this profound journey of loving you, you might feel the desire to mix something sweet and watch it rise. It happens to the best of us. It will bring you closer to yourself, especially when you have strayed too far away. And if a cake feels a bit overwhelming, make muffins. You can always shift a recipe to align with what feels good for you. Make it yours.

back to you in the studio

I am inviting you to get curious, lean in, and listen to what is hungry inside of you. The language, imagery, recipes, and remedies in this book are a powerful kind of recovery. Let it be a medicine for the way you think, speak, dream, and manifest your life. When you choose language that aligns with your heart's purpose, it clears the path for you to get closer to yourself.

Take this language with you. Try it on, fake it till you make it, give it a whirl around the block, and before you know it, you will come to know it as a part of you. Throughout these pages, I am on repeat with how *being and doing can live together* on a Tuesday at two in the afternoon, or

really anytime of the day or night. I am shining the light on what might be standing in the way between you and the phenomenal life that is right here, waiting for you. I have found a path to wholeness alongside the overflowing laundry baskets, the packed to-do lists, the deflated bubbles in the bath of dirty dishes that are waiting for me as I write these words to you. You are inside every moment of your life. Your hunger for yourself is your invitation to love and wisdom and infinite possibility. I am inviting you to devote yourself to YOU. This is your chance, my beloved reader: bring all of you here. Let's do the good work of finding what you love so you can light the way to your fullness and heal the world inside of you. As you heal, the world heals.

Welcome to this world inside of me.

Don't ask me if I am hungry
Don't ask what I want to eat

Feed me your heart
Feed me what you love

Then nourish me
Nourish me all the way

The tea you love and how you take it
The dinner you ate last night
The take out from that place you love
around the corner

All of you inside this food
That is what I want
That is what I hunger for

I am hungry for you

I am hungry for your story
Inside your home
Inside your laundry
Inside your body
Inside your kithcen
Inside your day-to-day, nonstop-life

Let's fold these clothes

Let's take out the dishes

Let's go deep and laugh about the mess

I will turn on the fire for one more cup

Warming the kettle

I invite our elders in

Learning how to listen

I offer myself over

What do we need to know?

Tend

They will say

Tend

They will sing

Tend to your hunger

Then feed those you love

with what you love

Then feed the world

permission:

the act of allowing someone to do something, or allowing something to happen; the act of permitting, formal consent, authorization, the approval of a person in authority.[1]

nourish:

to provide with food or other substances necessary for growth, health, and good condition. To enhance the fertility of; to keep a feeling or belief in one's mind, typically for a long time. To nurture, rear, encourage, cherish, feed, sustain and support.[2]

become:

to begin to be, grow to, turn into, to come into existence, to undergo change.[3]

YOUR PERMISSION SLIP

Stain, spot, splatter, mark, blemish, and smudge love, soup, cake, and quinoa all over these pages. Really make this book yours—the journey, the pages, the whole thing. This is for YOU! Your *yes* here gives you all the freedom and permission to make your way to YOU.

This book is your compass, your guide, your map, your Waze to you. You can write everything down in the margins, along the binding, next to the recipes, so you remember what you found, unearthed, dug up, ran across, pinpointed, hit on, recovered, and reclaimed during your journey. I love the idea of you opening to a random (not random) page that has wise guidance for you in a moment or every day. I also love you bringing this book with you all over the house, the city, and the world. It can hang out with you on the kitchen island as you wait for the kettle to boil or at your bedside as you melt into one of the stories or poems as a salve before you fall asleep. There is so much to dive into, steep in, swim through, thrive with, grow alongside, and rise into your greatest life. You can always begin again, which is really just continuing where you left off, even if you might have thought you were done. Every page is an heirloom, a legacy, and a language that supports healing your lineage. Sign this with your soul. Keep a pen, a felt-tipped, Earth-friendly Sharpie, or some other kind of writing implement that feels good in your hand, as you will want to see where your signature takes you. Your yes might move you to take notes, jot down *me too's*—highlight, bold, and underline all that wakes you up inside.

This permissions slip gives _____ (your name here) all the permission that ever was and will be to venture forth on this phenomenal, powerful, lovefest of a journey to becoming herself/himself/themselves again and again forever and ever, and so it is x x x

Sign Here:

"Life's work is to wake up, to let things that enter into your life wake you up rather than put you to sleep. The only way to do this is to open, be curious, and develop some sense of sympathy for everything that comes along, to get to know its nature and let it teach you what it will."[4]

Pema Chödrön

part 1

waking up
the stories we carry

invitation

Waking up to our lives is brave work. It is the work of beginnings and mornings and mothers and journeys. It is also the vulnerable terrain of belonging and survival, conditional loving and lineages of old values passed down and never healed. Waking up is the beginning of your journey here. It is the start of a practice to see and feel the places inside of you that go hungry. This hunger lives and "thrives" in these old stories you may carry. Like I shared in the introduction, you might have no idea that you are hungry until you find yourself in a space of beauty and permission and loving warmth that allows you to feel something profound opening inside you.

This awakening can also happen inside the unknown, while awaiting a diagnosis or moving through a painful time in your life. Whatever invites you closer to your truth is also calling you to wake up to this deeper place inside of you. This is where your pain lives, and inside this pain is your wisdom. As you make your way to this wisdom, you will meet it

as your guide, your mentor, and your elder. It will teach you how to see and soften, clear and tend, move and be moved, nourish and honor all of you. Over time, you will come to know this wisdom as you because it *is* you. There will no longer be anything in the way to divide or separate you from your deeper self. This is the beginning to your becoming.

In chapter 1, you will open to your taproot story. This is the story of how you woke up in the mornings of your childhood. This kind of story is full of sensorial experiences like hearing the sound of the garage door closing, smelling coffee brewing, or feeling the sun's warmth making its way into your bedroom. Your childhood mornings modeled what beginnings feel like and what you needed to do to be loved, belong, and make it to the bus on time. These morning memories also hold many of the embodied senses you carry today. These moments and how they integrated into your body as a child laid the groundwork not only for how you wake up to your life today, but also how you live it.

As you move into chapter 2, there will be a few stories to bring you to a more

intimate awareness of your remembering and the feelings that might arise there. You can lay them out in the
sun, hold them in your hands, stir them into a soup—
all with the intention to create a safe and loving place
for you to feel your pain. This is a place where you and
your stories can be seen, heard, and felt. As you explore your feelings here, you can bring them into the
kitchen. You can bring everything that is alive in you
into the kitchen. Whether it is grief, guilt, shame, or
sadness—all of your suffering can step right onto your
kitchen island. We will turn on the fire. We will peel,
chop, and stir all that has been in the way to nourishing you. Slowing yourself way down to the pace of
this moment will be your best friend here. Be gentle,
love. There is no rush. It takes courage to slow down.
The courage you cook up here will be your offering
to yourself throughout this healing journey. You can
warm your love tea and gather your fierce and tender
heart as you begin to make room for what needs to
come through and what wants to let go.

You will begin to see your new story emerge like a
bas-relief painting in chapter 3. As you bring yourself
to the remedies and recipes you are gathering, you
will begin to wake up to a new perspective. You are
birthing a new story. You are learning how to love you.
Your mornings are nourishing you. The quiet sacred-
ness inherent in waking up before the sunrise opens
your eyes to your breath, your body, your home, making your way to days you love inside a life you have
longed for. There are so many ways to wake up to
your life. Take my hand and let's go.

love tea

This moment, this tea, this warmth
is for you. Any moment of the day or
night you can begin again.
You can come back to your body.
You can feel your feet on the floor.
You can breathe in and out.
In and out. In and out.
You can find your way back to
LOVING YOU as you steep, stir,
and surrender.

tools

kettle or pot you love

tea vessel, cup or mug

steeper or sieve for loose-leaf tea

small bowl for your steeped tea bag
  and a place to rest the steeper

spoon long enough for the honey pot

cozy to keep the heat in and to rest
  your warm cup on in your hand

gather

organic black tea

boiling water

sage honey

organic raw cream, half-and-
  half, or any milk you love

a bowl or little plate you love

As you fill the kettle, you invite yourself into this moment right here. Slow it way down as you put the kettle on high heat. Reach for a vessel you love, a shape that fits your hand so you can feel the warmth in your palm. Making tea takes a moment, so you can too. Take this time to breathe; in through your nose and exhale through your mouth. Loosen your jaw and feel your body settle. Gather your tea, loose leaf or bag, and place it in your cup. I see you preparing this in your tea area. If you don't have a tea area yet, you can make one—a place where the honey, the spoons in a Ball jar or a drawer, perhaps the cups, and of course the tea, are all gathered for this moment. When everything is in the same place and accessible, there is an ease that permeates the experience, and your life.

Gather a spoon, the honey, and cream. Once the water boils, it is ready to pour in your vessel. Leave room at the top, and use your empty bowl to rest your sieve or tea bag after it has steeped. You want everything to happen in this one place. Making this tea will restore and reconnect you to beginning the day, again and again. I start the day feeling the LOVE right here with my body and this warm milky tea. I let my tea steep for a bit, covered with a tea cozy to keep the warmth in, as I like to use this time to sit and breathe—whether I bring my pillow into the kitchen or I go to the altar. Once the tea has steeped—about five minutes or so—I add honey first, then cream. I stir it all together. There is a particular color to the milkiness I love, so I look for that balanced hue. You will find the hue that works for you. Keep tasting and stirring and finding what you love. I love sharing this love with you. Enjoy, loves x x x x

mother story

We wake up to our mothers. They were the morning, the kitchen, the place we know as home. Your story begins inside your mother's story. Her story is the emotional terrain you were born into. This layered landscape is where you were nourished or not. It is where the felt sense for belonging and being loved either thrived or survived. Your mother was also the emotional blueprint for your sensory experience. For some of us, this blueprint was our father, our grandparents, or other caregivers. You looked to them for care and love, consistent connection and emotional stability. How they woke up in the mornings showed you how to do the same. Their *ways of doing and being* influenced how you met the day and learned to live your life.

Your mother's story and how she woke up as a child in her home of origin is related to your healing. Whether you know her story or not, you carry the parts of her story she didn't heal. All of our stories contain remnants and residues that were left behind, unhealed, from our ancestors. As you heal, it's important to remember that not all that you carry is yours—so much of it comes from your lineage. I also love to remind myself: there is only so much work one can do in a lifetime! This is also a great place to remind yourself that this is not a fixing journey; it is a healing journey. As you dive into your memories about your mother and how you woke up to her, you might feel less alone knowing that your stories and her stories are inside a powerful field of healing.

heart work

Welcome to your first heart work! This is where you can take a pause, warm your tea, breathe slowly, and dive a bit deeper—or just put your toe in to feel the waters of your story. These are moments of intuitive loving. You might read something here that inspires something else to open. Follow the desire to explore your story. That is what this heart work is for. It is a loving space to be with your heart and what it needs to tell you. Oh, and you can do this one every week for a year or every year forever. There will always be gold inside your words. Your word is gold.

eleven-minute timed writing

♡ Gather a pen you love, one that feels good in your hand and flows easily.

♡ Gather a journal you love, preferably unlined, like a sketch pad from the art store with lightly weighted paper, wide pages to adventure upon, and binding that easily opens.

♡ Gather a timer (preferably not your phone—an old-school timer).

♡ Be in a place you love that is also cozy and quiet.

♡ Give yourself what you need here: light a candle, climb under a blanket, wear cozy socks, or go barefoot under the trees. Take this moment to check in with yourself and feel into what feels good right now.

♡ Once you find your place, put the timer on for eleven minutes.

♡ Write at the top of a blank page: "In the mornings of my childhood, I woke up to . . . "

♡ And then goooooooooo. . . .
Don't stop writing until the
timer goes off.

♡ No thinking, pausing, or figuring
anything out, please.

♡ Your work is to keep moving
the pen on the page, writing
down every thought that
comes regardless of its truth
or what you think about it. You
are opening your heart-mind
connection as your hand keeps
moving across the page in flow.

♡ Let it rip! Be free! Have fun!
Laugh! Cry! Let yourself be in
the flow . . . and if you want to
keep going past eleven minutes—
do it! You are free to be!

♡ When you finish your writing,
take a breath, put the journal
aside, get up from your special
spot, stretch, take a walk, and
move your body. Allow yourself
to feel and move what is coming
through you.

As you return to your heart work, something new might have emerged. A new way of remembering your story. Bring this with you. Let it be seen and heard. Write it here along the bind. Allow yourself to be here with it. As you remember more of your story, you might feel into your child self and how you learned to survive or belong or be loved. Be gentle here. Perhaps your memory is not as clear as you would like it to be. You might not remember anything. That is okay, too. Whatever is alive here, be with it. Maybe there is a voice in you that thinks this is a bit crazy. Perhaps you don't want to blame anyone or say anything because *nothing was wrong, everything was fine. They did the best they could with what they had.* Yes! They did! Healing your legacy is not about right or wrong. You are not blaming or fixing or investigating. Your healing is not about what *they* did. Your healing begins with where their stories left off. This is about YOU and your hunger to wake up to your life, which benefits your whole family line.

breaking open

Perhaps your story includes your mother's or father's job winning over connection, love, and time with you, especially in those precious morning hours. Or maybe you are feeling into the nonstop *doing* that so many of us experienced in our mothers. This ran them into the ground, mentally and physically. It also kept them from being with themselves. Underneath many of the stories inside *doing it all* was their hope and hunger to be seen, heard, and deeply loved. This inherited conditioning of serving the needs of others helped *earn their keep* so they could feel safe and secure. This "purpose" left them hungry, depleted, and lost. This is what was modeled—to find love outside of themselves. Perhaps you feel that if you were to stop your life for just one moment inside all you have going, you might just break . . . open. Breaking open could be the best thing that's ever happened to you and your lineage.

Light a candle to what is here. Ask the fire to hold this feeling with you. Bring this fire into the kitchen. You can take some eggs out of the fridge. Let them be out for a bit if you have time. You can put them in a bowl, a basket, or a linen cloth. Gather the butter, too. The opening to your own deep love is waiting for you in the kitchen. It is rare to hear about a mother nourishing herself, healing in the kitchen, transforming the cycle of pain she inherited as she cooks for the family. This is what we get to do here! We are all mothering ourselves. No matter the story you carry and the pain that comes with it, you can bring it into the kitchen. Breaking open is a waking up. When I feel myself breaking, I want something soft, light, warm, and loving. As you discover the kitchen as a place for your healing with its fire and beauty and freedom, you might feel a longing to be in there more. Your life is just waiting to break open with you.

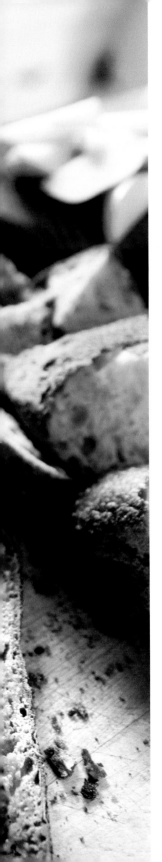

jam egg with toast

Eggs know how to break open. And with the support of the fire and the right tools, you can make something soft and delicious with salted butter, jam, and toast. What I love about this recipe is it works for all times of the day. You can have it for brekkie, lunch, dinner, or a snack on the wood board. . . . You just never know when you might want to break open inside the incredible adventure that is your life.

tools

stainless steel sauté pan

a small Pyrex or other bowl

a spoon

a small stainless steel
  spatula or wood spoon

a wide bowl

gather

salted butter you love

local organic eggs (always)

salt

cream (optional)

bread you love

local seasonal jam

your love

in the bowl

sautéed kale or any greens

avocado

honey

goat or parmesan cheese

nut or seed butters

thinly sliced heirloom tomato
  or thinly sliced figs

smoked salmon

prosciutto

As you turn on the stovetop, bring the dial to just before medium, place a little butter in the pan. While the pan is warming,

THE SUN
CAME OUT

gather your eggs and crack them open into the small bowl or Pyrex. Feel the shell inside of you cracking, too. You can put an open bowl near you for the empty shells. We crush them up for our chickens as eggshells help their beaks get stronger.

Look at those little suns! Like the yolk inside of you, bright and beautiful, these big yellow eyes are waiting to be stirred round and round—adding air to give it the breath and softness you will need. The more you mix, the more air they will receive and the softer they will be. Pour the eggs into the warm pan and bring the stove to low. Stir slowly with fork or spatula, adding a little salt or even cream here. You can also add shredded parmesan or peeled (with a peeler) goat gouda, or any hard cheese. There are so many delicious ways to soften into our lives.

Feel your feet as you watch what is raw create a shape that is light and airy. Toast your bread in the oven or on a cast-iron pan. Make sure your butter is left out of the refrigerator so it will be easy to spread. Bring the jam out and a small wood spoon to scoop it up. Serve in a wide bowl with any additions you love. Offer this goodness to yourself as you nourish the mother inside of you.

selfless legacy land mine

What is rarely acknowledged is how our mothers cared for everyone but themselves. This is what we saw, experienced, and, in time, embodied as the work of a mother. A mother's work is endless, exhausting and—wait for it—celebrated once a year in May. For many of us, our mother's "selfless silence" was the loudest voice in the room. Doing everything for everyone means that you not only have no time for yourself, you also have no time to *have* a self. Self-sacrifice continues to be admired today, even accoladed, like a badge you wear or a crest you paint at camp. Yet having no time for yourself is a land mine. And not having a self creates legacies of pain. I am not seeing the light here, are you?

You may not even know you are giving yourself away because it is so ingrained in you. We were conditioned to be self-less, literally to have no self. Once we become aware of this, we tend to run the opposite way to try and "heal" it. We run from where we first saw it happening: away from the aprons, the kitchen, the house, the relationship, when what we're trying to heal has nothing to do with any of these places or things. That would be easier. The healing is unraveling the stories that got stuck inside the foundational (and archaic) values of our forefathers and foremothers!

Getting to know who you are serves everyone you love in such a deep and rich way. This is an inside job. Deep breath here. Even when you claim your life as yours—you figured out how to have a tea, read a poem, and make an uninterrupted phone call all in one day—most of the time you lose yourself to the busyness of life and the responsibilities that are everywhere. Not having a self keeps you and your deeper wisdom forever hungry. So, as you head out into the world looking for yourself, like the llama looking for its mama, you end up walking around Target with that big-ass cart, trying to find something that feels like you in the widest aisles of a cultureless culture.

The truth is, you are a trailblazer. Many of us don't face the pain of this self-less condition until we become mothers or caregivers. When I became a mother, I had no idea how to keep myself close to me, to tend and love me as I made dinner, changed the diapers, and vacuumed the copious and never-ending blonde Labrador hair from the dark wood floors. Let alone keep a job and make sure everyone was alive in every moment. All I knew how to do was to keep going. To lose myself over and over again, hoping to be loved, seen, felt, and cared for by others. I had no idea that I could give myself the care I was seeking outside of me—that I had a body that was holding me, a self that loved me and a mother in the earth that was truly caring for me in every breath I took. This is where we go hungry! You might even have this awareness in your life, yet you have no idea how to change or move toward it. Your mother's love was given to you inside that old, conditional blueprint. No one knew anything different. The pain of her not knowing who she was got passed down to you like an unlit torch. And even without fire, that pain caught on and spread far and wide.

the sound of safety

In the mornings of my childhood, I woke up listening for the feeling of the morning. I would hear the roosters cawing in the Gap Band's hit song, "Early in the Morning." Or it was Luciano Pavarotti's "Nessun dorma" or James Taylor's "Copperline" or "Fire and Rain." My mother was the DJ to my nervous system. She had quite a range—both in the music she was playing and how fast or slow she was moving through the house. Upon waking up, I always heard her whirling like a dervish in the kitchen, the laundry room, the hallway, or the garage. She was up and ready to go with a cadence that would tell me the emotional temperature I was waking up to.

Yet there was consistency in the kitchen. Every morning, she would make her Earl Grey tea (some days it might be oolong, Darjeeling, orange pekoe, and every now and then, an English breakfast). Twinings and their paper colorway were a character in my morning play. My mother would scoop a teaspoon of sugar in the raw into her porcelain teacup. I could hear the conversation between the spoon and her cup all throughout the house. All of her sounds were like a siren song informing me of what shape I might need to shift into in order to survive the morning with ease. The sounds of my childhood kitchen were part of this song. My mother expressed herself, whether it was rage or joy, through these sounds. Even now, the clanging of pots and pans jar me. You will hear me say, even if I am alone, "Sorry! That was so loud! Didn't mean it!"

Does this bring up sensory memories for you? Was it loud in your home when you woke up? Did you wake up to music, or silence? Or the alarm clock blaring? What was happening for you inside your senses? Did you wake up feeling like you were already late? Are you always rushing now? Use your pen or any writing implement that you love to jot down a few notes here. What were the senses you relied on the most to inform you? You can write a list here in the margin of the book. Whatever comes up, go for it. In time, you can connect these experiences with how you feel in your life today.

Nessun dorma means "let no one sleep." The song is an aria from the final act of Puccini's opera *Turandot* sung by Prince Calaf, who falls in love, at first sight, with the cold yet beautiful princess as she beheads her rival suitor. It is just a Tuesday in Boca Raton, Florida. I am probably putting on some black eyeliner in my bathroom mirror and picking out what I'm going to wear to school. The aroma of breakfast permeates the house as golfers drive by in their carts and the sun rises in Her full splendor. Even with everything happening inside of her, my mother always made me something warm to eat. She made sure I was fed.

My mother carried hungry stories from her childhood, too. She was the oldest of four siblings and became a young caretaker to them while her mom, my nana Pat, worked the night shift at the hospital as a polio unit nurse. Before my mother got married, she began to *rewrite* her story by converting to Judaism and living in a different financial bracket than the one she came from. She was like the Energizer bunny— so much doing without any being. Her doing had this event-like energy that never ended. It was an embodied angst that I inherited. In my teen years, my mother went back to school, graduated from college, and continued on to receive her master's degree. She was ravenous for knowledge and learning everything she could—yet I didn't see her integrate it into her *being*. It remained topical and separate from the rhythm of her day-to-day living. Perhaps this was her *deeper work*. Maybe this is how she was trying to find herself. Because of her hunger and the pain she carried, I never knew how peaceful or painful the day would be. It was never just a Tuesday. As I got dressed and ready for school, it always felt like we were getting ready for something much bigger.

In nourishing your stories, you begin to listen to the pain you carry. As you listen, you can slow down and feel what is inside of you. You might begin to see where the pain has shaped you and what is most important to you now. Sit with yourself and take it all in. Ask questions and get curious. Are you integrating what you love into your day-to-day? Or do you hide it, hoping to get to it later? You can bring this inquiry into the kitchen. If you feel grief, bring it with you. If you feel anxious, bring it with you. You don't have to separate how you are feeling from what you are doing ever again. Let being and doing come together to hold you. Let your pain move through you, inviting you closer to your journey here. You can do this in the kitchen. As you nourish yourself with time, presence, and love, the grip of your stories will begin to release and let you go.

Your mother stories are potent places to heal, bursting at the seams, asking you to lean in to your heart and listen. As you do this, your stories will right-size themselves, settling into their proper dimensions. You are rebirthing yourself inside this new way of being. You might even fall in love with you.

hello, body!

three ways to invite yourself to wake up
to your heart wisdom

* Move toward your sneakers, put them on, and take a walk around the neighborhood. Even if you don't feel like it. See you how you feel after one minute of walking. Then check in at two minutes. Keep checking in with yourself and moving your body. You are learning how to listen to yourself.

* With a hand on the middle of your chest, listen for your heartbeat; this is the only playlist you need to hear.

* Wherever you are, take ten slow and deep breaths. Count as you inhale and count as you exhale, elongating the breath each time as you make your way to ten.

hungry mother

I am starving for this conversation to begin.

I want to ask questions, write lists, hear your stories.

I want to understand, get underneath, turn it over and see the other side

of this place where we are healing in our kitchens, with our bodies, for our lives.

Ode to the stories we carry.

Ode to the stories carried by our mothers, our grandmothers, our great grandmothers.

Ode to the bloodline laughing and grieving into the soup, the bread, the crumble, the cake . . .

This daily work of feeding each other, our kin, ourselves, is deep inside of us.

How we woke up, how we were fed and what happened

in the moments, the mornings, the days of our lives.

And now, we are nurturing, providing, gathering,

cooking, feeding, birthing, businessing . . .

Longing for the ground, for something deep and warm and rooted.

We return to this mother place again and again,

Hungry to be heard, seen, felt and nourished.

Hungry to stir, fold, mix, and rise.

Hungry to make room for wisdom.

Creating tradition from scratch to begin, again.

April 2009

chapter 2

the pain you carry

When people share their experience, strength, and hope, something profound happens. You feel their vulnerability and their courage. And inside their vulnerability, you can find your willingness to heal. It is a collective experience. We are not meant to heal our pain alone. It does take your *yes* to show up and keep going. In time, you will find others saying yes too. This intimate terrain is transformational for everyone you know. Your yes to healing you heals the whole.

Vulnerable landscapes can open you to the warmest, most loving experiences. So, let's create a soft place to land, a safe space to be with your heart and the wisdom that will keep coming. Yep, your kitchen. What you do here will always hold your being. When you see what you love, you remember you, and in that remembering, you feel held. Find something you love and put it out where you can see it, and watch what happens. Your healing is happening no matter what you think! And it feels so good with a soup on low, offering that cozy aroma to soften you toward yourself again and again. Soup might just be the answer to everything.

chicken soup love

(with or without the chicken)

There are some recipes in this book that you can keep on low throughout the day, gently simmering all that is happening in your life. They are my go-to's. They support and hold me. They are deeply nourishing for everyone. Whether you know it or not, someone somewhere in your bloodline made the most amazing soup. The soup maker is also the doctor, healer, shaman, and soothsayer. This is not just any soup. Look at you becoming a badass healer!

tools

a big pot you love

a big netted spoon and/or a stainless
    steel colander with a handle

a soup spoon for tasting

a wide empty bowl

a ladle you love

you can always add water as you go, so
for now add just enough to the pot to
fully cover the chicken

gather

all the veggies you have, such as
    carrots, celery, green onions, leeks,
    fennel, celery root, and parsley

chicken broth or water and bullion
    (can be vegan or chicken or
    however you want to go)

salt

a local organic chicken that
    was raised with love

matzo ball mix (just in case)

First, I take a big pot out and put the stove on between low and medium. I gather the veggies that call to me. What feels good to your body right now? You can slow down here, asking yourself what you want. If you hear *go for all of it*, then do it! As I am peeling or chopping, I check in with my breath, see if I am rushing or gripping. I usually will need to bring my shoulders down from the ceiling. You can feel your body as you put your heart into the soup.

Breathe in slowly, breathe out slowly. Put the veggies into the pot as they are ready, then add broth or water and bullion. I love using good organic broth when I have it. Water with bullion or salt is great too. You are enough. You know how to do this. Call in your great-grandmothers. They have made this soup. They will show you the way. Use what you have. Don't let anything stop you.

Take some time to be with the chicken. Lean, heart and body, in to the experience. Don't separate yourself from this moment. As you rinse the chicken, offer gratitude for its sacrifice to nourish you. I like to give it a little salt bath and take off the fat from the neck and anywhere else you might see it. I love the fat, but too much can make the soup oily. As the water begins to boil, you can submerge the chicken in the pot. Bring it to low, put the lid on partially, and let it cook.

Place the wide bowl right next to the pot. After a good hour or two, take the entire chicken out with your netted spoon and put it in the bowl. You can put a linen towel over this and let it cool for a while. Keep the soup on low for as long as you need to. In time, when the chicken is cool, I get in there with my hands, taking all the bones out and adding the smaller pieces of meat into the pot. I eat a bit too. It is so moist and delicious from being cooked in the broth. Sometimes I will use some of this cooked chicken for a shredded barbecued chicken or a quick snack or meal for the kids, keeping the rest in the soup. Maybe I will put a bit on a salad for lunch. PERMISSION EVERYWHERE! You can keep the bones in a bag or glass container in the freezer for making bone broth in the slow cooker later.

Keep the soup on low and taste it from time to time. You can keep the lid on fully if you want, or slightly off with a tiny opening. This soup is even better the next day and the next. You can do matzo balls or ladle a little bit into a teacup, adding a scoop of avocado or some corn chips—even rice crackers if you love that softened crunch.

There are so many ways to nourish you as you make the room to heal and feel held by what you are cooking up for you and your family.

the pain of our stories

Setting yourself up to feel held inside your everyday life is essential to healing as a living. Now that you have your soup on low, we can begin again. You may want to know more about being held and what that feels like. It feels both light and rooted, like that feeling of being taken care of completely. It is a centered feeling, like that post-yoga-bliss vibe or after a really good dance party, or an enlightening run that moves you back into your body. This embodied lovefest is offered to you unconditionally by our Mama Earth. She holds like no other. Being held is deeply healing. It is solid, connected, and unwavering. You can create this feeling through the rhythm and flow of your day. It is an intentional practice. It is a part of your becoming as you live more aligned with your values. One of your values may be to feel your pain when it comes. You might have been someone who shoved pain down and didn't want to deal with it. A new value might be to bring your pain with you, to get curious and be with it for as long as it takes to heal. You can do this as you peel the carrots or feel your feet on the floor as your tea steeps. You can feel you as you make your way through the day. You don't have to separate from it or try to get to it later.

These shifts make a huge difference in your day-to-day life. Most of the pain you feel has been with you for a very long time. Regardless of how you were relating to it before, you are here, now, to recover what was lost. You are dusting off an old relationship where you coped skillfully, functioned highly, and behaved in ways that kept your light dimmed.

In the many years of circling, sitting, and being with women, I have found that we discover our truth inside the courage of another. Inside a safe container, listening to each other's stories, is where we meet ourselves. When you hear a fierce yet tender story, you might think, *That is my story too*. This *me too* is a medicine to awaken you inside another person's experience. Whether the story is the same as yours or nothing like yours, there is a heart knowing inside the pain that you can open to. We all know this deeply human place inside of us. Tapping into a sense of our shared pain and healing helps us move through our individual pain with more grace and ease.

When you share your pain, you make room for your wholeness to emerge. In one moment, you feel alone and scared, and the next moment you feel connected, seen, and heard. When we share our pain with each other, it is lighter to carry. Our lives become lighter to carry, and eventually, we don't feel that particular pain in the same way anymore. The shape and texture of the story shared changes through expressing our truth and offering it to the light. You no longer carry it alone. When you bring your pain into the kitchen, you transform it into something divine and glorious, like an olive oil cake with orange zest. This makes space for your wisdom to come closer and your cake to rise.

We all carry pain. We learn about our pain inside each other's pain. This is how we recover, mend, and grow. We all know suffering. This is our human experience we have in common, and it brings us together in ways we never knew possible. When we come together, we heal. Our pain is here to move us closer to our wisdom. As your walls melt away, the ever-emerging WE comes forward. WE is ME upside down. When I shift my ideas from *me* to *we*, everything changes for the better. Being inside the we is vital to healing you, me, and our Mother Earth. This is how our kindness, compassion, and empathy grow—they become the *me too medicine* we need for ourselves and for Her, our Mama Earth.

a mother-daughter morning story

I think of the mornings as frigid and empty: a Pop-Tart, defrosting the car, being late for school.

I think about my mom and her stress, which I now can recognize as stress. But I don't think I ever really recognized that our mornings weren't ideal, and the space was not nourishing. I think of her coming in from having a cigarette, dressed in a pantsuit, drinking her coffee, the kitchen smelling like nothing, maybe coffee; she definitely hadn't eaten. Nothing was ever cooking.

We know this story. Within a few sentences, we understand this scene. We are this single mother, rushed to get ready for work, surviving the morning and her life, *doing it all by herself.* We are this young daughter, struggling to make sense of her mother's hunger. She is rushed and running to work, to the cigarette, to everything that wins over this precious morning time—to share love, to eat something warm, to take a minute and check in with herself and her daughter. How would she know to do this? How would she know to be this? What is more important than feeling connected, loved, and nourished? When a stressful morning is considered normal, how do we find our way to love as the most important thing?

> It was always a battle of "What do you want for breakfast? Do you want cereal? Do you want some toast? Do you want a waffle? We are in a rush, you will be late, I don't have time for this, what do you want?" And I would say, "I am not hungry, let's just go." Or "Pop-Tart, I'll eat it in the car."

No one is being held here. The mother is ravenous in so many ways. Hence the daughter's hunger for food turns off, too. This is where the mother's pain becomes the child's pain. No one is there to nourish the hunger inside both of them, though this is the mother's work: to feed herself first, so the legacy can move forward in a nourished way. They are both hungry to be loved, cared for, seen, and held. There is no mother in the room. There is no culture to reflect them. Everyone is on their own, to fend for themselves and do their own thing.

> My regular weekly mornings were cold and stressed, rushed and uninviting. My mom would wake me up in a frazzled bad mood a lot of the time. She would yell, "You are a bear to wake up in the morning. Hurry up." I would get ready before breakfast. This was always our routine. Never eating first. Showering and getting dressed before food. I literally have ZERO memories of mornings with my dad. Empty mornings in my childhood.

This daughter can feel her mother's stress and how important it is, so she takes it on as hers. This is a mother who has lost her way, and now the daughter has no idea where to go. The rush doesn't sate the deeper hunger they are both feeling. The stress of the environment is winning over love. The broken culture they live in reflects their conditioning—the mother thinks she needs to live her life this way to survive. There is no room for feeling, or thinking about how this will affect her daughter now or in the future.

You might see this story in your story. Without blame or shame, you can feel this mother's hunger for herself and how it shapes everything around her. This is important to be with. This mother's hunger, neither nourished nor fed, creates more pain. She is not nourished by the work she is rushing off to do. When you bring her hunger into the light and hold it close, you can see how tender it is. You can see how this kind of hunger can spread like the unlit torch. You might get curious about this mother's pain and where it came from. You might wonder how she woke up in her childhood mornings and what her mother carried. What was winning in her home of origin? She might have been a child of the Depression or the era of the Holocaust. Perhaps she was trying to heal, rewrite, and move away from or change a pattern in her family. We don't know what we are actually "doing" until we slow it down and get curious about how we are running our lives. So many of us have learned that this is the way to success or paying the bills or "getting things done," yet there are bigger things being missed out on, like living.

How does this land for you? On its surface, this story might be nothing like yours, until you get a little closer. This separation and heartbreak and mother's pain is ours, too. We have seen this in our mothers. We are learning how to nourish the divide inside ourselves. This is how we begin to heal our pain. What is coming up here for you? Are you thinking about your mother and how her hunger shaped you? You can write it down here in the margins of this page. As you articulate this for yourself, you bring it to the light.

> I feel guilty. I feel sad for my mom. She was doing the best she could. I know YOU know that. So, I don't know why I feel like I have to protect her. Or why I feel guilt for talking about it. I think I just imagine her knowing about this conversation and how devastated and literally sick she would be over it.

It can be so deeply challenging to share your pain about those you love. This might be why you avoid *going there*. You don't want to hurt anyone. Perhaps you think you can control how they will feel. You might have been told that your actions can make or break a moment. Maybe you think that if you don't say anything, the "whole thing" will go away, or at least not bother anyone else—until your hunger bubbles up to the surface and the pain gets to a place where you *can't* live one more day like this. You want your mother to be okay, but really, this is about YOU. You want to be okay. Me too. And we are okay. The more you share and move the pain that's inside of you, the closer you move toward the true okayness that will heal you. In time, you become free.

heart work
becoming an offering

It is time to go outside or find a window to look out of. When it comes to pain, there is no better healer than Mother Earth. Oh, and time—time is also the greatest healer. Mother Earth knows all about our pain. Our pain causes her pain. Yet she keeps giving us air to breathe and fire to tend and food to eat. She is an unconditional mother. When I am in pain, I go to Her. When I am relieved to make it through an intense time, I bring my joy and gratitude to Her. I am in a relationship with Her. I invite you to do the same in this heart work and forever.

Begin to connect with Her in a way that feels simple and accessible. Baby steps. This is not a trip to Yosemite or the rainforests in Bali. You can feel a similar connection inside a daily practice with the sunflower growing outside of your window. It is easy to be in absolute AWE of Her and what She creates. You can start right here. Perhaps there is a tree on your street you love to look at or a view of the ocean you love to drive by. Maybe it is a hummingbird that visits you in the mornings. Whatever is with you, go be with Her. Go with your pain and bring an offering.

What is an offering? Simple is best. It is sweet water for the hummingbird. It is water or food and love for the tree. Ask Her to take the pain you carry. Walk barefoot in Her soil. Walk barefoot in Her sand. Ask Her what you need to know. And wait. Close your eyes and really be here with yourself and with Her. Visit this same place every day. Be with Her. Feel yourself with Her. This is sacred work. Wait and listen for what she tells you. It may take some time, but She will get back to you. The deepest relationships take time. You are learning how to be in relationship with Mother Earth. You are learning how to listen. As you learn this, your pain will change shape. It will no longer be heavy to carry. It will teach you what you need to know.

"No matter our pain or distress, all of life is in whatever moment we wake up to."[5]

Mark Nepo, The Book of Awakening

it's not an event, it's angst

The kitchen of my childhood was a container for all that might come through *her*—my mother's daily weather patterns. The constant feeling of an event, as if something big was about to happen, was embedded in basic moments like folding the paper napkins before dinner or putting ice cubes in the glass Pyrex pitcher of Bigelow teabags steeping with their white tags hanging over the rim. This untethered feeling was inside everything that was happening, when most of the time not much was happening.

There is a lineage of angst on both sides of my family line. We usually use the word *angst* as a noun, but in our home, it felt like a verb. Angst moves fast and works alone. You can barely catch her in action as she whirls invisibly around, making something out of nothing. There is always something to do, do, do. There is always a rush to get to nothing. Angst takes over any possibility for a deeper connection. Angst takes the air out of the room.

My mother's angst created an unsteady terrain for my childhood. The calm rhythm of what home could have felt like was constantly interrupted by this relationship with angst. It won over all the beauty she created and the abundance of her livelihood. This angst also served as the fuel that helped her out of the pain of her childhood and supported her to create a new life. The pain we carry and the relationships we have with it can be quite layered. Our pain can help or hurt us depending on our awareness of it. Pain is also a powerful catalyst. It can support you to move forward and begin to heal your life—even if that healing doesn't finish in your lifetime.

As you take these stories in, what emotions come up for you? The pain of your family line can be a healing—an invitation toward change. When you show up to your healing, possibility arrives. You begin to see things in a new light. As you step back and take in the wider view, something may shift. You know by now that jotting notes and making your mark inside this book is a request and a healing. You can always return to these pages and see how far you've come, and keep adding, too. Your healing is your legacy. It will feel so good to get things out and onto the page as emotions come up and move through you. When we begin to dissolve what is standing between us and our phenomenal lives, we make room for what is possible in our lives.

"Trust that your exhale will guide you forward."

Io Bottoms

healing in the kitchen

This feeling of angst is what keeps most people out of the kitchen. It perpetuates the forever-trending (and borrrring) stories of perfectionism and a whole slew of unhelpful ways of being. Many women would say they made a mental note very early on to never have people over, host a party or dinner, let alone cook. The way they saw cooking and entertaining modeled didn't look like something fun to repeat. This has caused so much pain. When you identify as someone who *doesn't know how to cook* or navigate their way around a kitchen, you are limiting what is possible for you. This limiting belief holds many stories of lack: not being enough or doing everything to serve others. So often, our relationship to cooking and the kitchen is based on an old, untrue idea or fantasy about what is possible in the kitchen.

Angst is a feeling of anxiety and frustration that isn't specific. Angst is anxiety that is mixed with fear. Often, angst refers to personal freedom.[6]

Cooking is an art form. It is a practice and a prayer. It is a healing. It is also a muscle. If it wasn't modeled in a way that makes you want to explore it, you bring that grief into the kitchen with you. Being in the kitchen is being in your heart's wisdom. It is intimate and nourishing, it can feel new and full of adventure. There is so much for you to explore, discover, and fall in love with in the kitchen. There is beauty, permission, freedom, and some really delicious food, just for starters.

Do you remember the kitchen of your childhood? Can you tap into the felt sense of that space? What was happening inside of it? Was your kitchen the unconditionally loving mother my mother and I longed for? My mother could throw a loaf of bread in anger or steam tomatoes with delight in her oversized All-Clad pan while singing to Anita Baker's "You Bring Me Joy." The kitchen would still be there, patiently holding us and all that we were moving through. The kitchen was available, present, and always willing to serve.

What are your memories of cooking? Did you wake up to something warm in the mornings? Or when you came home from school? Would you do your homework on the dining room table listening to your mom or caregiver making food for dinner? How did the kitchen, the aromas of food cooking, weave in and out of your life? Did cooking happen on a regular weekday, or was it only for a special occasion? Many women shared with me that the warm feeling of something good cooking happened on a weekend or a holiday, but the regular day-to-day was usually stress and struggle. What is true for you here? These are all important ingredients to how you nourish yourself today.

My mother and I spent more time together in the kitchen than anywhere else in the house. It was in the center of my childhood home and our relationship. When we were in the kitchen cooking together, angst didn't seem to get in the way of our connecting like it did in the mornings or when I would come home from school or after a night with friends. Being with my mother in the kitchen gave our relating a safer container. She loved to teach me what she had learned, and I loved to learn, even if her demand for my attention was sometimes a bit over the top, or the stories she shared took her out of her body. She showed me how to cook the recipes given to her by my Grandma Lena, her Jewish mother-in-law, and the challenges that came with those memories. She would tell me about the amazing women at the temple who shared their family recipes and the ways of "making the high holiday" as she was converting to Judaism at twenty-two years old. She would reminisce about her Grandmother Julia (my namesake) and the summers she spent at their home in North Carolina. Cooking with my mom always included her stories, which are my stories too.

Your grandmothers and great-grandmothers and all the women who came before you are with you in the kitchen. When you turn on the fire, whether you "know how to cook" or not, they come and hold you. You can call them in as you click on the stovetop, the oven, or even the rice cooker.

Even with all the pain, our ancestors held my mother and me in that kitchen. The love of our ancestors, no matter what their struggles were when they were on earth, is available to us at all times. They all tended fire and made food and cooked for their families. They come to heal with us in the kitchen. Our healing heals them. Our hands are their hands. Our ways of turning on the faucet, wearing the linen towel around our waist, or drying the dishes come from their ways, too. We are never alone in the kitchen.

latkes

My mom taught me how to use the Cuisinart. Many years later I learned that most people call it a food processor, but I will probably never call it that—"Cuisinart" was the way it was passed down, and it just feels right. My mom used it for so many things. She would slice hothouse cucumbers for her sweet-and-sour cucumber salad, mix the oily sweet dressing, or shred a million potatoes for latkes.

Of course, it doesn't have to be Hanukkah to make latkes. She made them all the time, and now so do I. Like all the recipes in this book, these are good for any time of the day or year! You might have heard about potato latkes, or pancakes, as they are sometimes called, from the story of Hanukkah—a story about light and abundance inside the unknown. It is a story about possibility even when you can't see it. It is about moving forward with fire and courage. The story transforms from thinking there is enough light for one night to discovering it lasts for eight nights. This teaches us to move toward the light inside of the dark. This is what all seeds do in the soil as they make their way to the sun. They grow regardless of what they know or how they feel about it.

During the time of my mother's converting, Lillian Steinfink would come from the temple and teach her how to make these latkes and other Jewish dishes too. She taught her this from her wheelchair. I never got to meet Lillian, yet she is the reason why these latkes are in my life and now in yours. Recipes and the stories they come with are powerful. May we remember and honor the journey of Lillian and my mom coming together as we gather our ingredients, learning new ways to nourish the pain and transform our lives. Thank you, Lillian and Mama!

tools

a cast-iron or stainless steel pan (the
   rounder and wider the better)
a peeler
a big bowl of ice water (optional,
   to prevent potatoes oxidizing
   or turning brown)
a few flattened paper bags on a
   big board or on the countertop
   next to the stovetop
a Cuisinart (or FOOD PROCESSOR!)
   or grater of any kind will do
another big bowl (or the same one you
   used before, emptied and rinsed)
a big wood spoon
a stainless steel spatula or
   stainless steel tongs

gather

vegetable oil such as sunflower or
   safflower, or olive oil works too
russets or any kind of potato that isn't
   too moist inside (you can also use
   ANY root vegetable to make a veggie
   latke, such as sweet potatoes, yams,
   celery root, carrots, beets, parsnips)
flour of any kind
one or two beaten eggs (4–5
   potatoes to one egg)
a bit of salt

in the bowl

sour cream
crème fraiche
goat cheese with sage honey
sautéed apples or pears
apple sauce

Start with your pan on low. Cover the bottom with a good amount of oil (you can always add more). Peel the potatoes, putting the peeled potatoes in a big bowl with ice water if you care about them turning brown (this is helpful if you are making a big batch).

Set yourself up with a brown paper grocery bag laid out flat next to where you will be frying. Make sure it is nowhere near the flame, and find a place to put your spatula; this is also a good time to turn on a fan if needed, or open some windows if that is supportive to you. Shred the potatoes. This is when the Cuisinart comes out. It is fast and helpful! You can also breathe and meditate inside a hand-shredded vibe, too. Scoop out all the shredded potato into a big bowl. Add flour and an egg depending on how many potatoes you have.

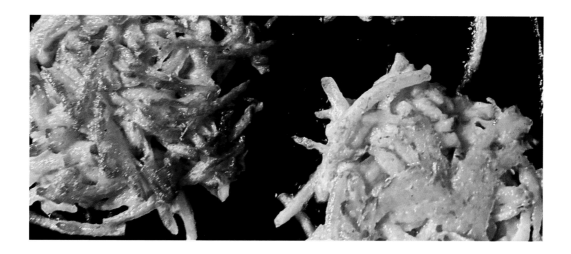

Slow yourself down here. Feel your feet and tune in to all the *rooted abundance* around you. If making latkes is new to you, breathe in the newness that is here and acknowledge how courageous you are to try something new. Your breath, the flour, and the egg are the glue that will keep the potato together while you fry the latkes in the pan. This is a great time to put the pan on medium to high heat. As you mix the potatoes, egg, and flour with a big wood spoon (I use my hands as they are the best tool I have!), you can feel into what you might need to add here. For eight medium-sized potatoes, try ½ cup of flour and one or two eggs depending on their size. Add some salt too. See how this feels as you put a finger-full scoop into the hot pan. Use your spatula to flatten it a bit, making a thinner patty—or what we like to call a LATKE! You don't want them too dry or watery. You want to find the middle way.

Let them fry. As they get brown and crispy, flip them with your spatula or tongs. When they feel done, bring them one or two at a time onto the brown paper bag to let the oil soak in. Use your spatula to remove the lingering fried straggler shreds as they might cause issues later.

You can plate these with a side of sour cream or crème fraiche and apple sauce OR get fancy with goat cheese, honey, and sautéed apples or pears. Or put a fried egg on top and call it a day! They are good no matter what you do. They are enough just as they are, and so are you. Enjoy, loves x x x x

showing up for you

Recalling your stories, feeling the pain that comes up, and awakening to the life you want to live is also a journey you take with your roots, your lineage, and your bloodline. It might feel scary and unknown. If you keep walking, the light will come. It comes with showing up for yourself. This is where the love for you lives. As you rewrite your story, you heal what your mother, and her mother, and all the mothers inside your family couldn't heal. You are being called to change the old patterns. And, like I shared earlier, there is only so much you will do in this lifetime, yet you will model something extraordinary. You will show the way to healing as living. Those around you will learn from you how to heal in their own lives. They will learn from you to never leave themselves. The invitations to change these patterns and the pain that moves with them are rarely on linen paper with gold lining and a fancy font. In slowing down, you will find your way. Claiming your journey here is trusting that you are held no matter what happened in the past. As you receive your own wisdom, you form a new relationship with yourself and with Spirit holding you.

My mother was my first home. She was the kitchen. She was the morning. She was my first relationship with my body. She held the first of many ingredients to my story. And now, as a mother of two, I hold these ingredients, new and old, in the pockets of my apron. Today, I wake up before everyone else. I wake up in the dark to me. I breathe and sit and warm the kettle. I meet myself where I am so I can nourish my famly from a more centered place. My mom is with me as I heal her story, *my* story, and cook up a new one for Beauty, Ocean, and all the mothers to come in this line. I invite you to wake up with me. I invite you to transform your pain into the healing you have been longing for.

ry for all the tr
ustr who craves
niness we all ca
hes the light and
in a life full of
who trusts my b
ns to be cozy ins
ounds of cashm
ting the broken
sharp needle i an
a hungry to sere

birthing a new story

The sun is rising. It is a new day. You have a new story to birth, a new way to wake up inside the morning. You hold the key to possibility. Mornings invite so many opportunities for love and nourishment. They are liminal spaces between dark and light, inviting you into a deeper connection with your life. This threshold is intimate and powerful terrain. You are transforming your story as you learn how to nourish your deepest life.

Here you are, at another beginning. Throughout your journey here, you will be waking up even as you leave the waking up section. You can begin again and wake up in every moment. Waking up before the house, or world, is essential to the practice of being with YOU first. You might be used to putting your family or your job or everyone else's needs first. What self? Who? Exactly. The energy of the first light of the day is a container for you. Listening to your breath first. Feeling how your body feels first. Being with yourself is where you begin. You were made for this.

hello, body!

waking up to you

Light a candle.

Breathe.

Make a love tea.

Breathe.

Slow it way down.

Breathe.

As you walk, feel you.

As you brush your teeth,
    feel you.

As you warm the
    washcloth to put on
    your face, feel you.

a below-the-neck conversation

Learning how to wake up to yourself is an embodied process. You are making your way toward your body with every step. There is nothing to do here. You are all body in the morning. Let yourself be all body. It is sooooo good when we allow ourselves to be who we are. No phone or email or any realms of the world outside will help you here. They will only take you further away. You are making your way into the world *inside* of you. Give yourself the time and space you need here. The other stuff will always be there. Living your life in a reactive state will always be there. Nourishing yourself is a below-the-neck conversation. It is not about what you *think* needs to happen or a reaction to what is happening outside of you. It is being with what needs to move inside of you.

Take a breath here. Let's slow this down. Waking up to yourself lives in your YES. It is not optional. You are not optional. Thinking about all the ways you'd like to change as you keep doing things the old way separates you from your body. It also doesn't feed the deeper hunger that is YOU. In feeding you first, you birth a new story. In making room to birth, your mind changes. You begin to be with yourself as a gentle, loving energy. No more critical analyzing or scanning the field for where you are "doing it wrong or setting yourself up for failure."

This is essential to your healing. When you slow down, you can shift your old survival techniques from analyzing to gentle curiousity. You can ask, *How am I feeling here?* If you find yourself resistant to the thought of waking up a bit earlier in the morning, you are not alone. You can invite the inquiry into why you have such adamant feelings about waking up early. Staying curious with your feelings is a way of nourishing yourself. You can operate from this new place inside of you. There is no rush here. You can be in the unknown as you build new scaffolding for your life. You've got this. You are taking the slow steps toward a morning that aligns with the hunger of your heart. One step at a time.

heart work

♡ Gather a marker or basket of colorful bold crayons or acrylic paints.

♡ Gather paper you love. Maybe it's kraft paper or card stock that you have kept in a craft box, or even a swatch of wallpaper you love. The only requirement is that it must feel like YOU.

♡ Write down a word that you are carrying for your journey here, a word that resonates with you waking up to your life!

♡ What was the word that just came to you? That was it! Write that one down!

♡ Then put it up where you can see it . . . perhaps on the window, wall, or altar above the sink or the ceiling above your bed or the bathroom mirror OR ALL OF THE ABOVE.

This is your remembering. This is what will remind you of your journey here. It might be easy to forget, especially in the beginning. It might feel new to make your way toward YOU. Creating little reminders for yourself is a loving way to support yourself. This is about seeing yourself and setting yourself up for success—every step of the way. As your word changes, put it up where you can see it. Keep moving with your healing. Stay with you. You are amazing.

As you wake up to your new story, you will feel yourself in the room—your feet on the floor, your breath moving in and out of your body. Your curiosity will support you here. It will be the bridge you build toward your self—beyond old judgments, fears, and comparisons. I didn't know about curiosity as a child, as it was not modeled. I still have to remind myself to breathe, get curious, and look around instead of reacting, protecting myself, and assuming I know what is coming. Those neural pathways are fierce and they were all great survival skills when we lived with tigers chasing us. I have found that taking the fast, fix-it-quick road leads to missing the magic that inspires me in the deepest ways. I am all in for the magic now, which means that most of the time I am in the slow lane. And when I forget, which is more often than not, I put my signal on and move on over to the right. The fast way seems to hurt. It takes my mind and my body with it, and then I can't show up for the people I love, especially me! When I slow down and get to know what is here for me, everyone benefits.

Speaking of slowing it way down, let's make something slow and sweet together. The beauty of using your hands with curiosity is that it gives you time to take in your life, to get closer to you.

sautéed
apple love

The physical action of peeling is a healing. Waking up to your new story is a peeling back of the layers, the rind, the protective conditioning that has kept you safe and sound . . . or has it? This recipe is for every day, just like your healing. I like to put the compost bucket nearby or the bunny bowl in the kitchen sink for the cores and peels. Set yourself up to make everything easier. Yes, *easy*. Say it with me. E-A-S-Y. Good work!

tools

wide pan you love
peeler
bucket or wide bowl for peels
another wide bowl for apples
bread knife or any knife
    you love for slicing
wood spoon or spatula

gather	in the bowl
butter	alone with a moat of cream around them
cinnamon	on top of oatmeal
apples	on top of latkes
	on top of roasted chicken, turkey, or other meat
	in a galette or tart

Find your breath and feel your feet on the ground. Place your pan on low heat with a tablespoon or two of butter and a few dashes of cinnamon. The butter will begin to melt as you peel your apples. You can feel into what you are peeling back. This can be very simple. It doesn't need to be a whole thing, if you know what I mean. The apples grew from a seed in a dark place. These apples are a part of your wisdom. They are also a part of a much bigger story, just like you! As you finish peeling each apple, you can place it into a bowl with water to prevent browning OR you can slice it thin and put it right into the pan with the melted butter and cinnamon. Allow ease to move you. There is nothing to do here. You are peeling a new story. You are melting with butter and love and spice. You've got this. Let the apples sit with the butter and cinnamon throughout the morning, creating an aroma to wake up to, or warm the house during a chilly afternoon. It also works as a sweet treat over vanilla ice cream. There are so many ways to nourish you inside your new story. Enjoy, loves x x x x

what are you waiting for?

Before I began this journey to nourish myself, I woke up to mornings that were cray cray for cocoa puffs. I was so hungry for change. I waited for it to come. I prayed, chanted the mantras, said the words, tried to believe I could change. I was waiting, wading, weighting—all the ways of *waiting*. What was I waiting for? I was waiting for everything. I was waiting for someone to take care of me. I was waiting for something to save me. I was waiting for something *out there* to do something *in here*. No one was coming.

Most of us carry some version of this waiting story. Waiting—for someone to rescue us, help us, care for us, do for us what we feel we cannot do for ourselves—is another form of conditioning we carry in our living. We learn this from our parents and elders. Waiting can be really good when it is intentioned, like anticipating a birth, death, and other major life events. It is when we fall asleep inside our waiting that our lives lose their lightness, freedom, and fierceness, which we need for birth! Perhaps this is what brought you here to take this journey to becoming you. Maybe you already got this, and you just want to make a few good cakes. Whatever brought you here, you are no longer waiting. You are moving toward you inside every page. Me too!

As you get closer to birthing your new story, you might find yourself wanting to go back to your old ways of living. You are looking at this week's schedule and wondering if you will be able to squeeze yourself in. You might think, *Yes to all of this, but I am just going to wait here for one more minute. Let me check the bank, the schedule, the emails, the family, and I will get back to you.* I get it. And I have seen this in all of us. Your *yes* for you doesn't live anywhere but inside of YOU. Waiting like this can be a good sign: it means something is about to change for the better. AND no matter what you do, you are loved. You can't fail in loving you. I know what it feels like to be scared of the unknown. You've got this. You really do. Waking up to yourself is the beginning of so much goodness for you and your life. Just keep moving forward. You are making room to transform.

finding me on the front porch

In the early days of motherhood, everyone in our house would get up at the same time. The kids would jump into our bed to play, wrestle, snuggle, and laugh. It was a lovefest filled with joy and laughter and lots of cuddles. I really loved these mornings—they are memories I will cherish forever. After that sweet goodness, I would step onto a treadmill of nonstop needs until I hit the pillow that night. I was slipping on banana peels all day long, trying to find myself and the pause button for my super-grateful yet fast-paced life. Remember that angst? Here it was in full view.

Someone offered me the idea of waking up before everyone else. My youngest was three years old, so that would be pretty early in the morning. At the time, I didn't have a lot of experience with things like "making time for me" or in how I mothered myself *and* my family. I still considered "me time" a luxury. And I was a mess. Nothing had worked so far, and I hadn't tried getting up earlier, so I was intrigued. I had nothing to lose except for sleep, which was already in short supply. In fact, some mornings I probably *was* waking up at the crack of dawn, but I would never think to actually get out of bed, much less to use that time to tend to my own needs. Who does that?

The next morning around five, I crawled out of bed and tiptoed up the stairs, hoping not to wake anyone. I was making my way to the front porch. I stopped in the kitchen to put the kettle on low, then gathered a cushion and a few books to take outside. I could feel how exhausted I was . . . from the last forty-something years. Settling on the cushion, the sun began to rise and I began to feel myself. It was so slight, yet I could feel my heaviness. Then a layer of grief came over me. There was nothing to do. No phone or sounds or distractions. I could hear the earth. The cars. My thoughts. *Oh, my thoughts!* (OMT) There was no camera on. There was nothing to show anyone. There was nothing to talk about. I closed my eyes. I put my left hand over my heart and started to feel myself breathe. I immediately started to cry. And even now, many years later, I still feel this tenderness when I center and go inside. It is this return to myself that brings me to tears.

I hadn't been with myself in . . . forever. It was loud, noisy, busy, and chaotic inside of me. It was a bit of a shit show in here. It was a land mine. It was a gold mine. It was all mine.

My body and the entire emotional symphony of longing and grief, shame and courage, trust and fear were all there with me on the front porch. And that was it—I made a commitment to show up every morning to myself whether I felt like it or not. I said *yes* to me and my crazy-noisy-chaotic-scared-sad-angry-loving-grieving body. I read the poems of Mary Oliver, Sharon Olds, and Naomi Shihab Nye. I woke up with Mark Nepo and learned about coming home with Thich Nhat Hanh and Ani Pema Chödrön. Their words were medicine to all the parts of me I thought were broken. Their words landed gently in the crevices of my broken stories like a loving salve. Their devotion to their highest service brought me to a deeper place inside of myself. There was nothing to fix. I was so hungry to be with me.

there is nothing to fix

As you create your practice, give yourself room to find your way. Gather swatches from all the stories you love that you have heard, seen, and lived. Let them inspire you to keep moving forward. The key is to keep moving toward yourself no matter what. Honoring your journey is essential here. Seeing yourself waking up in a new way is just as vital as the actual waking up. As you meet yourself in the early morning, be kind to yourself. Get curious about what you love and how you feel on your own, without anyone demanding anything of you. This can bring up a lot of uncomfortable feelings. You might freeze up or feel numb, not knowing how to be with yourself. You might feel bored not doing for anyone else for a few minutes or months. You are changing a pattern. You are finding your way to you. You are FULL of amazingness; you just haven't had a chance to get to know yourself.

As you honor whatever comes up here, you are also learning how to value yourself. You are looking at life through a new pair of lenses. Over time, you will see many things in a new way. Honoring comes from *the heart mind*. You can feel this as your mind bows down to your heart. It is an awareness with a wider, more expansive view of living than our mainstream one. This is a place of slowing down. It is quiet and private and grounded. It is not loud, trending, or on a billboard. It lives beyond the three steps to healing that your mind craves. Don't get me wrong, I love those three steps—I've included them below! The mind is an incredible notetaker and your body is an exquisite memory holder. And as your forehead bows to the ground of your heart, you will come to know the body as your healer. Your heart is your elder. It was the first organ to be fully developed in your body. Everything that makes you *you* grew after your heart was wholly formed. Your heart is your greatest wisdom. In the ways of honoring, the heart and mind come together. They are together as one, guiding you as you become.

hello, body!

being with your heart mind

* Make a sacred place on the floor to lay out a blanket, sheepskin, or yoga mat. Find your way to the floor. Stretch your body in all the ways it wants to move. Stay close to the ground as you move into Pigeon Pose, Happy Baby, or just stretch your legs from side to side. You know what to do. Make your way to Child's Pose. This is where you can rest your forehead on the ground with your knees wide and your belly letting go between your thighs. Let yourself be here. Breathe slowly. Allow your body to let go. Loosen your jaw and sound out *haaaaaaaaa* through your long exhales.

* Draw a warm bath with Epsom salt, a tiny scoop of coconut oil, and some essential oils like eucalyptus, rose, sandalwood, or jasmine. Ask the water to cleanse you. Bring honoring to your body. This can be a quick bath. Don't wait until you have time. Make the time to be with you.

* Put on music you love. Light a candle on the kitchen island. Make a cake.

you are your holy work

You are your holy work. As you birth your new story, you move toward the YES inside the whole of you. Your mother stories are out, the pain is moving through you, and you are honoring yourself for possibly the first time in your life. You are waking up to you. You are also coming to understand that every-thing is here *for you*. It is not happening *to you*; it is happening *for* you. When you look around, you might not see this yet. You are learning to look inside.

   In the forest, when the taproot is nourished, everything grows. It doesn't matter the species or the type of tree—the taproot makes sure that every root is fed. This supports the growth of the whole. You are a yes for this taproot-level work. You are the trees, you are the forest, you are the earth. In waking up, I am inviting you to create a life that is aligned with every part of who you are and what you want inside your life. In the space you are making here, miracles happen. You can bring this holy work to the fire, move it with your body, heal it in the kitchen as you become you, over and over again. You are nourishing the taproot, the mother root within, so all of you (and US) can grow.

What is a life that nourishes your hunger? Perhaps it is a life where cake is made on the regular. This is our first of many cake recipes in this book. I love how the individual parts, the wet and the dry, come together to make something moist, giving, and sweet. Cake is proof that as you nourish the divide inside yourself, you will rise lighter and more delicious! Start with heating your oven to 350 degrees.

olive oil cake

tools

8- or 9-inch circular stainless
steel cake pan

parchment paper

KitchenAid or hand mixer or
whisk and a big bowl

wood spoon

cooling rack

toothpick

gather

2 cups flour (I use King
Arthur gluten free)

1½ cups sugar

1½ tsp kosher salt

½ tsp baking soda

½ tsp baking powder

1⅓ cups olive oil (get the best you
can as it can make the best cake!)

1½ cups milk

3 large eggs

1½ Tbsp grated orange, lemon, or any
kind of citrus zest (I love orange)

¼ cup fresh orange juice

Oil up the cake pan, and line the bottom with parchment. In one bowl, whisk the flour, sugar, salt, baking soda, and baking powder. In the base of the KitchenAid or a bigger bowl, whisk the olive oil, milk, eggs, zest, and juice. Add the dry ingredients to the wet, and mix until just combined. Pour the batter into the prepared cake pan. Bake at 350 for one hour, until the top is golden and the toothpick comes out clean. Transfer the cake to a rack and give it some time to cool. Then enjoy for dessert, breakfast, or anytime.

Enjoy, loves x x x x

the whirling dervishes

I wake up to the whirling dervishes

inside my solar plexus

I can feel the gentle wind from their skirts

passing thru my breast cavity

I can feel the rush of their dance.

This is my invitation

to slow it way down.

As my pelvic floor vibrates

from this archived angst

inside me

I breathe

I walk to the fridge

I gather four eggs

I notice their bare feet

dancing on my rib cage

I hear the stories

inside their soles

As they turn

And turn

And turn

Inside of me.

I crack the eggs

I whirl the whisk

I am meeting them in their dance.

And in the distance,

I feel my body

And the body

behind my body.

I see my mother

who can't see me

This is an old story.

It is a Thursday at 8:22 a.m.

I am so high from this mint tea

I didn't get in Turkey.

I softly scramble the eggs

I toast the sourdough

I spread the salted butter from France

I juice the Olinda oranges.

And one by one

I turn

And turn

And turn

These stories inside me

into a soft place to land.

I lose the to-do list

I throw hope into the fire

I begin to see beauty everywhere.

April 2016

"Most of our journey is looking for ways
to discover who we already are.
It is no secret that slowness
remembers and hurry forgets;
that softness remembers and hardness forgets;
that surrender remembers and fear forgets."[7]

Mark Nepo, The Book of Awakening

part 2

turning on the fire

haaaaaaaaa

invitation

To turn on the fire is to come home to yourself. You are true radiance, and the fire is a reminder of this truth. A flicker of light ignites the elements of change kindling inside of you. As you walk deeper into this book, you may step out and wander into the unknown. The fire holds your hand in the dark, softening the corners of doubt, clearing old landscapes of fear and lack that can lead you astray. You move forward as the fire melts you down to your essence. Some days it can bring you to your knees, which brings you closer to the earth. You lay your forehead on the cold, moist soil, bowing to Her, listening for your heart wisdom. The fire says: *Gather around so we can burn what no longer serves.* The fire says: *I am here to hold you as you heat up, cool down, die off, and rebirth yourself.* The fire says: *I am here to show you your light, to inspire you to tend and transform.* Ode to the fire and the medicine ways of change it brings.

The fire meets you right here: as you call in the directions, wisdoms, and ways. As you open to your lineages and legacies. As you honor the land that holds you. You will come to know that you are fire as you sit by the fire, stand by the oven, and light the candle on the kitchen island. The fire will tell you what it needs you to know. As you learn how to listen, you will change your mind. As your mind changes, you will move closer to healing the Earth. Thank you, fire.

candle, kettle, oven, firepit, slow cooker, whatever it takes . . .

We want to gather by the fire even if it's a toaster. We want to be close and warm together. We yearn to feel the love inside an aroma of roasted root vegetables or something softening in the slow cooker. In chapter 4, we will light the fire in your busy day-to-day life. This will support you to return to you, in the present moment. It is so easy to get taken by the day, the needs, the to-do list, and all the ways we are shaped. Lighting the fire returns you to your breath as you integrate *doing* and *being* inside the day. You are making your way closer to your body and the wisdom that you are. In lighting the fire, you inspire a space to be, a place where you can make sound with your breath. These are loving ways to ground yourself, hear your heart mind, and offer a rhythm that supports you to move around the kitchen and the world.

As you clear what is in your way, you walk deeper into the rich terrain of ashes and renewal. In chapter 5, you learn about tending the fire as an offering, and a ritual for remembering. Remembering requires presence, which serves everything you are growing. As you tend, you move closer to the life you long for. Transformation is quiet, profound, and usually under the radar. You are changing in every moment. As you invite this sacred practice of turning on the fire into your day, you are creating a life that brings you home to your becoming.

chapter 4

lighting the fire

Lighting the fire invites the love in—and the spaciousness in which to access the love. Lighting a candle or warming the oven can hold you as your heart moves into the center of the moment you are in. The warmth initiates this place in you that calls for a deeper sense of yourself. Starting the day this way sets you up to see and feel you first, and then to light the way toward your truth. Even if you have forgotten it for one minute or many years.

You can do this in the morning or anytime that calls for you to begin again. For me, these times are throughout the day when a shift is happening with the sun or the energy of the house. I might want support in transitioning to the next moment, so I light a candle (I am known to light a few at a time!) in the early morning, mid-afternoon, and early evening.

Lighting the fire is a practice. So is finding your breath. The fire sustains you inside all your *doing-ness*. It is called *being-ness*. The flame of the fire insulates this sacred feeling as you do your life. Fire offers you this in abundance as it clears and purifies the space you are in, all the transitions of the day and your life.

morning fire

It is 5 a.m. My eyes open to the dark. I gather my glasses and sweater from the side table and try not to trip over Sammy Bear, our German shepherd. I tiptoe quietly, choosing the floorboards that don't squeak as I make my way down the hall, then downstairs. I strike a match and light the beeswax pillar on the dining room table. *Ease for the day and all beings everywhere.* I go from being completely in the dark to seeing one glowing line, and it lights my way to the kitchen. With matches in hand, I light another candle on the kitchen island. *Peace in my body and the world.* This lights up a cake plate of yellow peaches, white nectarines, and a small pink bowl with two Bosc pears. I am making my way to the kettle. *Thank you, fire.*

As you wake up to the dark of the morning or a season in your life, the fire will light your way. You can give language to this element of fire and offer an intention for the flame to hold for you. You are entering into a relationship with fire. As it lights the way, it radiates through the house and beyond. What can you offer to the fire? It is doing the work of elements, work we can't understand yet we benefit greatly from. It is like a slow cooker: you put all your ingredients in, and over time, it melds the separate parts together into one. This is what the energy of fire does. It is generous and abundant in its ability to transform. As you light this fire, you are the sun rising for your body and your home. Intentioning the fire is not an event. It is a way of healing, and being. It is quiet and profound. It also lights the way to the kitchen.

You can feel your feet on the floor as you turn the dial on the stove and hear the click, click, click as the gas meets air, inviting you closer to yourself. This is a miracle—you have lit three fires and haven't even brushed your teeth! What is happening here? You are creating a space of light inside the dark. You are here to wake up in a new way, to find your breath, to listen for you and your body. Lighting the fire brings you closer to you. You breathe in through your nose and exhale with a quiet *haaaaaaaaaa* out of your mouth. You can feel your belly loosen. You are not in a rush. You are giving yourself time. You are giving yourself presence. It is 5:30 a.m. The phone is nowhere

to be found. You are just here, being. Lighting the fire invites you to do this, to just be. All of you is welcome.

Whether you wake up scared, paralyzed by anxiety, or filled with ease—you can light the fire and feel it change something inside. It is in this quiet place, before the world wakes up, that you can hear yourself—your needs, your breath, your body—letting the fire hold all of you. You can stretch by the stovetop. You can be slow. Slower. You reach for the Ball jar of oatmeal and pour it in the rice cooker. You turn the boiling kettle on low, you make a love tea; you are learning how to be with you. You are learning how to love you.

oatmeal in the rice cooker

Waking up early in the morning is essential medicine. It also supports you in getting ahead of the rush. We intend no rush, yet life is in session, and we know it can take us from ourselves in a split second. This is what I like to call *getting ahead of it*. This is also a *doing-to-be* remedy. Oh, it feels so good to get ahead of it, "it" being all the needs of your life, your family, and the world. Many of us feel late the minute we wake up. This morning practice nips that right in the bud, and so does this recipe. The rice cooker (or slow cooker) is like having an extra mother or grandmother in the kitchen. It is another incredible fire holder. To have food ready as your family, friends, or YOU wake up feels like such a deep caretaking. To get ahead of it is an intentional practice. It is also a mindset. It heals the *waiting* you might get caught inside of, along with the sticky feeling of hoping to be taken care of. This recipe (and this journey) is your caretaker. You are taking care of you as you hold your body by the fire with your breath, some cinnamon, and love.

tools

rice cooker (or slow cooker)

wide wood spoon

a Pyrex measuring pitcher

bowls you love

spoons you love

gather

salted butter

1½ cups of organic oatmeal (I love
  Bob's Red Mill gluten free)

cinnamon (a couple of dashes)

½ tsp or a small capful vanilla extract

dates, dried cherries, or
  dried or raw berries

3 cups water and/or almond
  or other milk

in the bowl

organic cream or half-and-half

maple syrup

soaked and peeled almonds

the sky is the limit on toppings

Turn on the rice cooker or slow cooker and place a scoop of butter in the vessel. Add the oatmeal, cinnamon, vanilla, dried fruit, and water or a mix of water and almond milk or any kind of milk. This is a 2-to-1 recipe, which means for every one part of dry ingredients (1 cup, ½ cup, etc.), the liquid will be double regardless of the particular measurement. Many grains are 2-to-1, like white rice and quinoa. You can put the rice cooker on the "rice" or "on" setting. You can let the oats be in there for as long as you need. Give yourself time here. Give the oatmeal (or any grain) time to be in the cooker for 30 minutes or more. They will continue to cook and soften. You get to do this, too. You can go breathe, walk, stretch, be with you. As the kids get up or you feel your hunger, you can create a DIY buffet on the island. Add a little organic cream or half-and-half, a little maple syrup, nuts, or whatever toppings float your boat or oat, in this case. Enjoy, loves x x x x

haaaaaaaaa (a forever heart work)

As the oatmeal cooks, you can breathe. Breathing is powerful medicine. It reminds you that you are alive. It also reminds you that you have a body. Inhaling through your nose is called inspiration. You inspire yourself as you bring life into your body and expire as you breathe life out of your body. It is pretty phenomenal, and we do it all the time! Yet are we really being with our breath? No wonder there are so many books on how to breathe. Whenever you feel you have lost the way to your breath, haaaaaaaaa can help you find your way back. When you inhale slowly through your nose and exhale the sound *haaaaaaaaa* from your mouth, the sound's vibration stops that endless loop of thinking your mind gets caught in throughout the day. Haaaaaaaaa invites your mind to settle, right-sizing all that is happening around and inside of you. When you exhale the sound *haaaaaaaaa*, you can visualize your mind dropping the mic toward your heart. This serves to slow everything wayyyy down.

Breathing with intention is another way to honor yourself in the regular moments of the day. Feel your feet on the floor. Envision roots growing from the soles of your feet into the earth. Light a candle. Begin another moment in a sacred way. You don't have to wait for the perfect moment to do this—I don't see it coming. Do you? You are growing a muscle to feel you inside the day. You are beginning to do this as you make the lunches, prepare for the day, grab all the things you will need for the car. You can *be* this as you *do* your life.

I have found that many of us love to finally sit down, close our eyes, and breathe. You might at first resist making the sound that *haaaaaaaaa* requires. This is another invitation to light the fire and listen to what might be in your way. You wanna try it with me? I can tell you from experience that once you do it, you will love it. I mean, really *do* it. Not a hum or a low, under-the-breath vibe, but a deep breath in and out, bringing the low belly with you and then letting goooooo. As it becomes a part of your day-to-day, everyone you know will start doing it too. It is free, and you can bring it with you everywhere.

heart work

♡ Light a candle on the kitchen island or another altar.

♡ Breathe in through your nose and out through your mouth.

♡ Center here for a couple of breaths.

♡ You can put your hand on your midchest or heart chakra area.

♡ Take your time.

♡ Loosen your jaw, relax your tongue, maybe swallowing to relax your throat too. Really get into the relaxed jaw mode. You can even stretch your mouth big, like a lion's breath, to come back to a more loosened state.

♡ Breathe in through your nose again, open your mouth slightly, and begin the sound *haaaaaaaaa* as you exhale.

♡ You can put your fingertips on your jaw to help massage the area.

♡ You can also do this all over your face—essential face massage medicine!

♡ Connect to your low belly as you inhale.

♡ As you exhale with the sound *haaaaaaaaa*, bring it to the place that is tight or in need of this breath.

♡ Visualize a loop or sphere of breath around you, this larger body of breath holding you.

♡ You can take your haaaaaaaa breath on a walk, to work, in the car—everywhere you go.

The vibration of *haaaaaaaaa* supports the mind to come home to the body. This is actually your superpower. The more you use it, the more powerful your practice becomes! Another sound might want to come through—maybe a sound that feels more aligned for you. You can make this yours as you allow your voice, breath, and body to be moved by this healing. This is another way to light the fire inside of you. It is another way for you to connect with the deeper essence that is you and your wisdom. Hold nothing back. Your haaaaaaaaa breath brings you back to you, every single time. Haaaaaaaaa says, *Let's open and release all that is in the way. Let's become the way.*

feeling you first

When you light the fire in the morning and breathe, make a tea, and begin to get ahead of the day, you feel yourself first. When you feel you, you remember you. You value you. You fill your own teacup first. This is simpler than you might think. You don't need to go to Bali or India or on a vision quest to check in with yourself throughout the day. (I mean, it is a great idea when it happens . . .) Even if you do fly far and wide for a retreat, at some point you will have to come back to your day-to-day life. Healing inside your life is transformational. It is the path you make toward yourself through repetition and practice and a deep devotion to you. This becomes one of the greatest things you can do for your living. It is also a tending. Lighting the fire reminds you to check in with you, and if you feel lost, it helps you find your way back to you. Feeling your body in the room no matter what is happening around you supports you to be present with what is right here. This is healing for everyone.

Waking up before the house, before the sun, before everyone's needs, changed my life. When I finally slowed down, I could see how I was merely surviving my days. Living was a honed and sculpted survival technique. Maybe from the outside it looked lucky and easeful and fun, but inside, I was barely holding on. I decided to burn the forever to-do list and the fantasy it perpetuated—that once I checked everything off the list, I would be free. Are you feeling this, too? How did my precious, amazing, one-of-a-kind life become a to-do list? Another ode to angst and all the ways we run from the intimacy that this life has for us.

Freedom is an inside job. It is not something out there. It begins with checking in with yourself. It begins with lighting the fire, finding your breath, and feeling your feet. When you nourish you, you become what you need. You become full, light, and hungry for more.

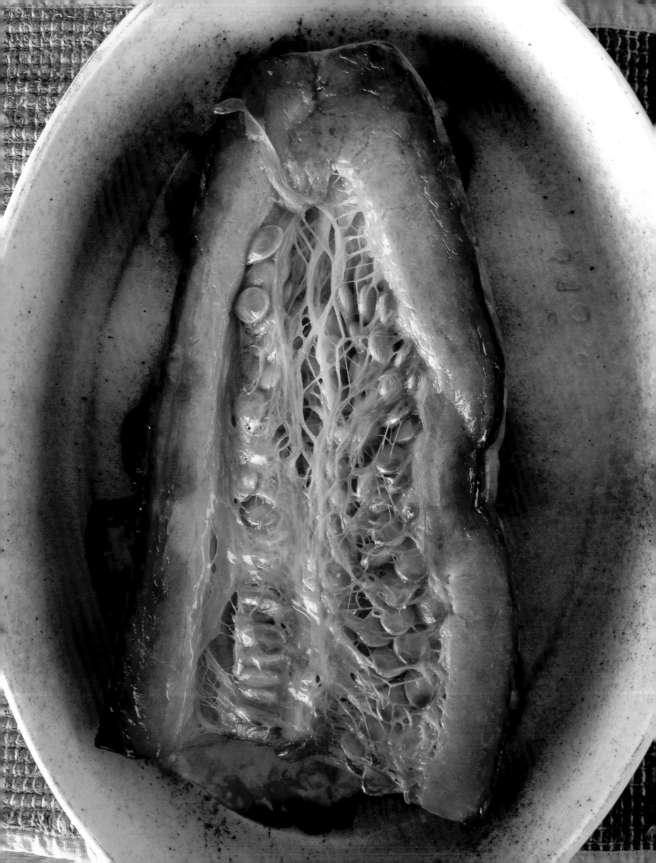

roasting root vegetables

& softening where you come from

I am back in the kitchen, dipping a long spoon into the sage honey, watching the golden thickness wrap around the spoon, like the liquified Murano glass out of the ovens in Italy. I see my mother's hands in mine. I feel the sweetness inside this moment. I pull the soft grey linen towel off the oven handle and tie the corners of it around my waist. I think about my Grandma Lena and the apron she wore. I think about all the aprons tied around all the waists of my ancestors. I feel my feet here as I move to the next thought, which is about dinner and who will be home. It is still the morning. I am also thinking about my client who is coming over in a few hours for a session and how the aroma will support our work together. I open the fridge to gather parsnips, carrots, Japanese turnips, and all the radishes in the drawer. I reach for the big baking sheet, olive oil, and an open bowl of salt. I turn the fire of the oven on to 375 degrees. I want to get something softening. It is not an event. I am getting ahead of it.

tools

stainless steel baking sheet or pan

ceramic casserole dish

pie plate or any oven-safe dish

linen towel

gather

olive oil

veggies you love

a wide bowl for scraps

salt

love

Find your breath here. Roasting veggies is one of the simplest, most beautiful offerings. They last a few days, and you can always have them with other meals, or as a snack. Local and organic taste the best. They also don't have such a thick peel around them as they haven't endured too much travel. I generally don't peel locally grown veggies because usually they were just pulled out of the ground and their skin is thin and tender. If that is not the case, peeling is a good idea, and you can put the scraps in a wide bowl for the chickens or compost.

Your love for you is everything, so bring it with you as you pour the olive oil onto the baking sheet, or casserole dish. If you rinse the veggies, you can lightly dry them by shaking the excess water off as you put them into the pan. The water is okay here as it will steam and cook in the oven. Massage the oil onto your veggies, add a generous pinch (or more) of salt. You can always add more later. The main thing here is to make sure the smaller things cook together, and the bigger things cook together—separately. So, carrots and parsnips are good together. Japanese turnips and radishes are good together. You can cut them in half or leave them whole—they are good either way. You can put the timer on for 20 minutes and check in on them at that point. You can do another 20 minutes depending on what you are roasting.

When they are done, you can take them out to leave on the counter or stovetop with a towel over them. You can also serve them as they cool. When they stay out, you might find they get eaten quickly throughout the day. Food out is food eaten, which is a beautiful feeling of abundance! Keep them out so everyone is fed in their own way. We are all hungry. Especially when gorgeous roasted veggies are out on the counter, waiting for us to gather around and feel that wonderful sense of home.

clearing and offering

As your roots soften, you might feel a desire to get closer to those you love. You are making room as you light the fire inside your life. At the same time, you are shining the light on what no longer serves.

You can do this on retreat, in a circle in the backyard, or on a Tuesday in your kitchen. Fire invites you to lean in closer to your life. It softens what is hard and lightens what is heavy. Fire changes the cellular formation of your thoughts, emotions, and the environment you are in. It turns solid into liquid, water into air, batter into cake. It can also burn the house down if you fall asleep to it. Fire transforms the way we live. It lights up what you couldn't see . . . until now.

Fire is a relationship, an offering, and a sacred healer. You can go to the fire in fear, anxious in every way, nauseous, scared, or feeling any and all of the uncomfortable feelings that come through a body. Fire is also a beautiful place to offer your thanks and deep gratitude for getting through a difficult time. Fire helps you move what you are carrying. Fire is a below-the-neck conversation.

What do you offer a healer like this? I will give you a hint—there is not just one answer, and it doesn't involve a checkbook or your Western mind. This is an inquiry. An inquiry is a place to sit, be with, and ask another question. An inquiry is to be inside of an offering, fully present. What could I possibly offer this fire? What I offer will never be equal to what it offers me. This is true. And this truth keeps the relationship aligned. Our relationship with fire is a place to honor and value. The healing that happens here is wide and deep and not tangible yet real and true. Knowing our place in relationship with Mother Earth is so vital to healing the whole. I honor the fire as it holds me. The fire meets me right where I am and offers me everything I need in the moment. It brings me home. As I blow out the candle or turn off the oven, I say aloud, "Thank you, fire."

"Offering is a mindset," says my teacher and elder Deena Metzger. There is no separating from ourselves in relating to the wisdom of the earth—only honoring and offering and being in the inquiry. We are the earth. When we deeply understand this, we begin to live in the "we" mind. When you live aligned as an offering to the earth, you are in a more "we" mindset. When you heal, you are lighter to carry. Can you imagine how that must feel for Mother Earth? You can move through your life, and truly care for her. I feel all that I carry, and I give it over to the fire so I can be lighter on Her. I offer my hardness and heaviness. I offer this anxiety and fear. I offer deep gratitude. I offer not knowing anything every time I am in relationship with fire. I offer listening. I offer my hunger to learn how to listen. All of this can happen with a cake in the oven and the kettle on low.

hello, body!

~~~~~~

a space for healing with fire

* Creating an altar is simple and doable; you may already have one (or ten) depending on how many places you light candles in the house and the kitchen.

* Your altar can begin as a beeswax pillar or a votive in a handmade holder with a few matches nearby.

* You want to give your candle and matches a place to be held. The matches can be in an open bowl, or perhaps you decorate the box and put a word you love on it.

* Altars are intentional spaces that hold what you are healing.

* Altars feel like you; they are a place for you to remember you.

* Altars manifest what we are calling in.

* If you are calling spaciousness into your life, don't clutter your altar. You can also write the word "spaciousness" to place on your altar.

* If you are calling in peace, let your altar feel peaceful.

* An altar is a living space, as is fire, and in your relationship with it, you can bring it a daily offering.

* An offering can be rosemary from the yard, a healing stone you found on a walk, anything that has meaning to you.

* You can offer the fire your heaviness; you can write a few words by the candle; you can heal in any way that feels like an invitation to come home to YOU x x x x

tending to transform

Tending a fire requires you to slow down and see what the fire needs. You can walk around it, look at it from all sides, and decide whether it needs air, space, kindling, or more wood. You can do this in a firepit, with a candle, or with the oven in the kitchen. You can also tend to the fire inside of you this way. To be aware of the fire and how it burns is to be in conversation with what the fire needs. As you tend this fire inside of you, you become more present with your needs, which you might have forgotten you have. You invite yourself closer to living the life you long for as you tend the house, the family, work, and what's for dinner. This begins with how you tend to yourself.

It takes courage to make room to hear yourself and truly listen to your needs. Most of us don't do this until there is an emergency. We wait for the ambulance to arrive to finally get on board with that voice inside of us that has been asking us to stop, to pause, to rest. This is normalized in our self-less culture. It is considered normal to not ask for support until you are dying, or close to it. Even as I share this, you might have this internal, conditioned gauge that is set for when it is okay, or barely comfortable to ask for support. Borrrring Story Alert. So many of us were shaped this way, so as not to be a bother or make a big fuss. This evolved into not being able to feel ourselves or being frozen when something comes up inside our lives. It takes a radical kind of intimacy with yourself to take the time to get to know what you need, let alone ask for it. It also takes fire to thaw out the numbness and return to our reawakened self. This is brave work in a malnourished culture. Meeting yourself by the fire can connect you to this place of being and strengthen the intuitive muscles that you may have ignored, denied, or not even known were here for you. Getting closer to the fire invites you to be with these places inside of you. This begins with making a fire.

My husband, Joshua, is one of the best fire builders I know. He makes a phenomenal fire. He is also really dedicated to tending a fire. He has offered his recipe for building a fire as your next heart work:

heart work

Building a fire is a mindful act. It requires an honoring of space, air, preparation, slowing down, and heat. First, you will want to gather all the right ingredients:

♡ Small kindling, like dried twigs and small branches, that will burn easily.

♡ Paper or fire starter (never use charcoal lighter fluid); paraffin-coated starter is my preference.

♡ A shovel or something to dig a small hole with if you are outside.

♡ Have two or three sizes of logs, from small to large; you will want to start small and wait for the heat to build before adding the larger logs.

♡ Tobacco or dried sage to offer to the fire.

♡ A lighter or matches.

♡ A tool to move the logs and coals around with, like tongs or a pitchfork.

Step 1: Create a small starter fire: make a hole about twelve inches round, and put the paper (lightly crumpled) inside. If you are making a fire somewhere you can't dig, then make a wood cabin with small sticks by stacking them crisscross like in Jenga . . . then put your paper inside that. Do not add anything else other than some small (very small) kindling on top. This is the patience/space and air piece—go slow.

Step 2: Light the paper and watch as it slowly starts the kindling. If you go too fast, you will suffocate the fire. It is alive and needs air and room to get going.

Step 3: Watch it grow, and then add very thin, small pieces of kindling, letting them stand upright as much as possible—do not lay them flat or they will suffocate the fire. . . . The air lifts the flames and the heat from below.

Step 4: It is critical for the fire to grow from the bottom. You are creating a base with hot coals before you add logs—go slowly and build with kindling.

Step 5: Once you see the fire beginning to heat up, lean two logs on each other, making a teepee shape over the flame.

Step 6: As the fire grows on the logs, lean more logs on them. . . . Tend the fire as necessary and remember to set fallen logs upright to channel the air from the heat in the core of the fire.

Step 7: Offer tobacco as an offering to the fire and the ancestors. If you wish to write intentions on a piece of paper or leaves nearby—you can offer what you are letting go of or what you are calling in. Everything you offer here is in service to the whole—you and the earth and your ancestors are inside of a powerful conversation. This is bigger than you think. It isn't a fixing. It is intangible yet very real. It is an offering to your healing. This is your Tikkun Olam. This is your mending of the world. When you heal, the world heals.

tending as an offering

Fire, not tended, turns to smoke. Many of us witnessed the women in our families—our mothers, aunts, and grandmothers—dissipate their energy like a slow dying fire as they tended to others. They would laugh and say, "I am running on fumes." They *lived* as though the house was on fire. Their tending was a conditioned response to their capability and identity. It was fueled by needing to prove and belong and feel safe. Yet when you are running on fumes, you are living without any fuel in the tank or nourishment in your body.

Tending fire and being with your healing in a consistent way does not live in the realm of urgency or quick fixing or an empty tank. *It is a long game*, as my friend and coach Rachel says. It took me a long time to understand what she meant. Your healing in anything—a marriage or a business or your life—is a long game. Tending is also not fast. It is daily. It is repetitive. It is based in ritual. It nourishes and sustains the foundation of your life. It creates and reshapes what you value. To tend fire is also to be an offering to the fire.

You do, do, do and rarely if ever stop to be with yourself, let alone slow down to notice the present moment. You may ignore your body, push down your feelings, "live" your life until you achieve this or get that, and eventually, you burn out. So many of us are living this way because this was modeled to us. You separate from yourself to get through your life, and in this separating, you forget who you are and what you are moving toward. Your body will have a lot to say about this—and maybe it is already speaking loud and clear for you to hear. This is where anxiety, panic, and chronic skin issues live, along with the entire universe of autoimmune diseases. As you bring this language, and these ideas, close to your heart and lean into the felt sense of *being an offering*, you invite yourself to a deeper place in you. You can return home again. As you tend, you begin to see the stories that continue to run you. How you care for and listen to these stories

Tending: to pay attention, apply oneself; to serve, listen, await, watch over; to take charge of as a caretaker; to cultivate, foster, manage; to stand by.[8]

will take you to the next level of how you are living. How you care and listen will transform your life.

When you feel into the idea of you and your life being an offering, what shifts inside? This is a good place to take a Ha breath. Haaaaaaaaa. Offering is being in right relationship with your values and what really matters to you. To be an offering, you will have to change your mind. What could change your mind? You can jot down any thoughts that come to you right here in the margins of the book. These are your field notes. A shift in your language makes space in your body. A shift in your body makes room for a new perspective. It might bring you to that wide and deep place your life is calling you toward.

tending as a remembering

When you take the time to tend, to the fire inside of you or to the pantry, something changes. You can feel this change as you return to yourself. Tending is also a remembering. Remembering your needs can feel vulnerable. It can seem easier to support everyone else and get to you later. You keep living for others until your body starts to get loud and fierce with pain or dis-ease. In remembering, you can begin anytime, and you can always begin again. The beauty of remembering yourself is that you can do it all the time. You can set yourself up to remember you along with the day-to-day things on the forever to-do list. In time, the *"to-do" list* becomes the *"to-be" list*. This can happen in the kitchen. So many of us go into the kitchen with old stories like the ones we talked about in the first part of this book. The angst or the obligation wins over feeling our feet on the earth or making a warm tea to nourish our body.

When you remember, you can connect to yourself as your stories are being revised. You can light the fire with your intention and feel your relation to everything as you peel the carrots, warm the pot, and chop the ginger. You are the carrots being peeled, you are the ginger being chopped, you are the pot being warmed. Remembering is the remedy and ritual for connecting to yourself and the earth, to your body and the fire.

Remembering can also make you hungry! Let's feed the revolution inside of you! Cooking food with fire is transformational. As you hold the wood spoon and stir these simple ingredients together, you transform too. As the fire softens what was once raw and hard, you can feel this softening inside of you. When you are connected to everything you are doing, you begin to feel this deeper sense of being. This is where remembering lives. It is also inside this bright, velvety lovefest of a soup.

carrot ginger soup

tools

a pot you love

a wood spoon

a bowl for peels and nubs

an immersion blender or a Vitamix,
    or any blender you have

gather

olive oil

organic ginger

organic carrots

water

salt

love

This is one of those recipes that, once you do it, you will know it by heart. It will become yours. I learned it from my dear friend Haidee, who cooks with love everytime she turns on the fire. Turn the stovetop to low and gather a pot you love. As the pot warms, pour a bit (1 tablespoon or so) of olive oil into it. Chop up the amount of ginger you love. Peel the ginger first, then add the bit you chopped to the warm oil. As the ginger steeps and softens, begin to peel as many carrots as you have—let's say two bunches, which is about 8–10 carrots. Chop the carrots and await the ginger aroma, which will be your cue to throw the carrots into the warming pot. Add water to just cover the carrots. You will bring all of this to a boil and then down to a slow simmer, leaving the lid on partially, letting everything get to know each other.

As all the parts soften, the aroma will permeate your remembering. This takes a good forty-five minutes to an hour. You can leave it warming longer or turn off the stovetop and keep the lid fully on. Once it's cool, make sure it is soft and ready to go into the blender. Once blended, taste the velvety lovefest that is your remembering. Salt to taste. You can add so many things to this, and yet the simplest way of this soup is the best offering. Enjoy, loves x x x x

grateful grieving

Remembering yourself can also bring up feelings of loss or grief. When you feel so far away from yourself for so long, it can feel overwhelming to come back to you. This is where healing in a collective is so powerful. Through the incredible work of Brené Brown, Gabor Maté, and other trailblazers, grief is finally being recognized as a normal feeling to have and carry with you inside the day. Thank Goddess because I was really getting lonely in my dingy for one in the middle of the ocean. Now that grief is somewhat trending, you can talk about it and bring it with you everywhere. You don't have to hide that you are grieving or sad as you feel grateful and joyous, too! We are multifaceted human beings. We are everything in every moment. This IS normal.

You may never have thought grief and the kitchen could go together, yet they do; they were actually made for each other. Grief heals in the kitchen. It transforms by the fire. When you invite grief to be with you, which is healing in itself, you can nourish your grief as you feel yourself putting seaweed, dried mango, and a cheese stick in your child's lunch. You no longer have to separate your grief, or any feeling you are carrying, from what you need to do.

Grief is a very special guest. And it doesn't necessarily know when it is coming or going a lot of the time. It is so vital to invite your grief in to play, cook, walk, and breathe with you. I am speaking more to the daily griefs we feel yet rarely talk about. Grieving in our everyday lives is normal. You can grieve the moments, as they will not be here again. You can grieve who you were ten minutes ago. You can grieve your growing children and the beauty of the day. You can also be deeply grateful as you grieve. You can feel this as you harvest the mint in the back yard, putting your feet in the soil or walking fast through the city. I call this way of being *grateful grieving*. I am inside this feeling every day. You might be, too. When we name our feelings or just that we are feeling, we offer them over to our healing. You can be everything because you already are. You are everything. And so is this cake.

ginger cake

Cake can also be a grateful grieving. Haaaaaaaaa. Perhaps you are feeling lighter. You are beginning to feel the need for a cake: a ginger cake to integrate this new way of digesting your life. It is so vital to celebrate the medicine of the fire. When you light, tend, and transform, you begin to feel yourself and your life as one. You are connected to YOU! You are devoted to remaining present, no longer leaving yourself. You can make a cake in joy. You can make a cake with sadness. Bring your grief to the batter, let it get moist and rise. Grief is one of the best things you can bring into the kitchen. You are healing. You are rising up to meet yourself right where you are as you make something sweet and full of love. Start with the oven at 350 degrees.

tools

8- or 9-inch cake pan

parchment paper

a mixer with bowl

another bowl (for dry ingredients)

measuring spoons and cups

rubber spatula

toothpick

linen towel

cooling rack

gather

2 Tbsp salted butter, softened

¼ cup sugar

1 large egg, room temperature

½ cup molasses

1 cup gluten-free King Arthur flour, or any all-purpose flour

1 tsp baking soda

¼ tsp ground ginger

¼ tsp ground cinnamon

small pinch of salt

½ cup hot water

Butter the cake pan, sides and center, line with parchment paper, and put to the side. Beat the butter and sugar in the mixer for 1–2 minutes. Add the egg, mix, then pour in the molasses. In a separate bowl, mix the dry ingredients: flour, baking soda, ginger, cinnamon, and salt. Place the dry ingredients into the base of the mixer with the wet ingredients, and add hot water to the mix. Mix well. Using your spatula, pour and scrape the batter into the pan and put it in the oven for 25–30 minutes. Do the toothpick test in the center; if it comes out dry, do one more to double check. When it's done, take the cake out of the oven and let it settle for a few minutes in the pan. Then take the cake out of the pan and place on the cooling rack.

You can make a little whipped cream to top it off! Pour 1 cup of organic whole cream into the Cuisinart or a wide, deep bowl to mix with a hand blender. Add a few drops of vanilla and a sprinkle of powdered sugar, maple sugar, or monk fruit sugar. Mix until peaks just begin to form; then put it in the fridge until the cake is ready. . . .

This ginger cake is so good for any season, and of course, it calls us inside during the fall and winter months when we are transforming and might not even know it. Enjoy, loves x x x x

thank you, fire.

unraveling

Letting all the seams go:

what I should be
who I thought I was
what I need to be

I am unraveling

Pin me up
each meridian
take me out of the oven
and let me cool down

I am making room
on the sides of this pan
pull that seam
watch my dress fall:

I am in bed with my lover
on a Monday at 10 a.m.
Yeah that's right

I am healing
I am making room
I am leaning in

I am so hungry for
my breath
my body
this fire
What was
ain't working

Let's talk to each other

get curious

be of service

hug it out

Let's try this warrior costume on

one last time,

so we can unravel it

at the seams

A marriage of old shapes

doesn't fit me anymore

Let's get under this fat mess

dig up the rotted roots

fire up the rusty pots

smell the aroma of your needs

roast the beets

make another tea

and unravel.

May 2014

you have a body
the middle way

"In the beginning, we all danced."[9]

Gabrielle Roth, Sweat Your Prayers

invitation to the middle way

You are becoming someone who warms love tea as you gather language that is aligned with loving your life. By now, you have ventured through some of your stories, turned on the fire, and made a cake or two. I hear you haaaaaaaaaing around the house, allowing yourself to heal. You have arrived at the middle of your journey. Here in the middle way, you can turn and look behind you. Notice how far you have come. Then turn toward the path you are making, right here in front of you. The terrain inside of you is transforming. You are safe to feel whatever needs to be felt, and with this safety comes the freedom to move. You can take your shoes off and put on your cozies. You are waking up in the dark of the morning, and turning the treadmill of your life on low. You are gettng out from behind the desk in the middle of the day to moooove your body. You are getting out of your own way. You are becoming the middle way.

As my friend Emilia likes to say, "The party starts tonight!" And, *tonight* is right now!

This section is one big, luscious, heart-work-hello-body lovefest. You will not need your mind or any thoughts—unless they are open and ready to love yourself even more! This middle way is dedicated and devoted to YOUR BODY. You will notice there are no recipes or heart work or hello, body! exercises here; instead, you are focused on being with your body and moving your healing to integrate all that is here for you. The sections titled "Move You" are spaces to put the book down and be with your body. As you follow along, you'll find ways to make this space your own. THIS IS FOR YOU. The only thing you need is your body and a willingness to explore what is here for you. You can read it all at once and then begin to integrate it throughout your days.

These next few pages are for moving and being moved. The difference between talking about the body and moving the body is like the difference between talking about Uruguay and moving there. Very different. Moving and feeling are essential ingredients to your becoming. Time will not just show up for this. "Later" usually means "never." The perfect time is now. We have found ourselves here together. Let's do it. Your showing up here will change your life. There's nothing special you have to do or be; moving happens in a million different ways. You can stay in the clothing you are in, you can move in the shower . . . you don't have to make this an event. Actually, please don't make this an event! You can move one small muscle on your face, your hands, one finger, your feet—you don't have to move everything at once. In a moment, we'll begin by lying down. Meet yourself where you are and *just beyond yourself* too.

As you move, you will make space in your heart mind. This can be an active place for ideas and thoughts to emerge. You might want your journal or this book nearby to write down what comes up, if anything. This happens to me all the time. Once I move my body, everything changes, particularly my thoughts. As I make room, I feel lighter. Even if it feels like I am moving through thick, wet mud in the beginning. What does your body need you to know? What do you need to tell your body? Let yourself goooo. If you have a body, you can move your body. Nourish yourself here in the sparkly warm water of this middle way, where you can feel and float and fumble your way toward yourself. Take in the beauty of you. There is nothing to get to. You are right here. You are right on time. You've got this.

All you need is

Your body

And a willingness

To explore what is here

For you.

"Whatever I am feeling is where I begin."[10]

Gabrielle Roth, Sweat Your Prayers

move you: moving your thoughts to the side

We are going to begin with moving your thoughts to the side. Oh, and please don't wait for a calmer moment to do this. I don't see it coming—do you? *Now* is the new *later*.

* Find a spacious area to be with your body. A space you love, in your home or outside. You are looking for a good floor area, any floor: kitchen, living room, toy room, whatever it takes.

* As you make your way into this carved-out time, visualize your thoughts like hungry, wet cats.

* As you take your time transitioning onto the floor—visualize these noisy cats. See yourself at the oven, warming their milk, scooping out some food for them, possibly cracking a raw egg into the bowl—I hear they love that.

* Visualize placing their bowls and a few sheepskin cushions into the little spare room on the side of your mind. Those wet cats will follow you in as you set down the bowls and settle them in. Close the door gently.

* Keep envisioning this scenario as you make your own area on the floor with a yoga mat and maybe a candle on the altar, creating a cozy, loving space for yourself.

* Now it's just you and your body!

* Light the candle and find your breath.

* As you lie here, you might hear one of the cats crying or another thought wondering if you put enough milk in the bowls. . . . Whatever the thoughts, you can introduce them to your breath and let them move with your exhale.

* Inhale gently through your nose and exhale through your mouth, opening your lips slightly and dropping your jaw, relaxing your face and allowing yourself to be here with your breath. You can sound out a haaaaaaaaa breath here, too.

* Soften your face and all the faces you wear. Let your face go as you let go of your thoughts and the sounds around you.

* As you feel the hard floor, soften your body to meet the hardness. Your breath is the bridge as you slow yourself down to be here.

* You can feel your journey and the journey of your body. Only you can do this. Feel into the power of your YES here for your body.

* Allow yourself time here, time for loving you.

You have a body. Your body is a magnificent mystery. There will always be more to unknow. It is impossible to know all that is happening in your body in one moment. There are so many layers, systems, energies, cellular structures, and stories folding and unfolding into each other like egg yolks into the batter of a flourless chocolate cake. This folding takes time. And perhaps you feel that in your healing. Maybe you want to know everything. You want to figure it all out. You were told that knowing everything will keep you safe. You were told that knowing is the only way to success, belonging, a life of okayness. Well, I am about to tell you the next essential step to your journey is to surrender knowing. Knowing will not feed your

hunger. Knowing will not cure you of this deep longing to truly become your beloved. Your body is a holy world of magnificence. Your body is the forever invitation to feel you. Your body is the forever conversation to become you. When you move your body, you make room for your wisdom. Your wisdom lives in the depths of the unknown.

this is a below-the-neck conversation.

when you move your body, you change your mind.

when you change your mind, you transform your life.

let go of thinking your body.

let go of figuring out your body.

invite curiosity into your body.

move you: stretching your stories

As you begin to feel yourself wanting to move, start with stretching; it is the bridge to the next moment. Give yourself the time you need to stretch and feel your body today. Transitions are vital in movement and in life. My yoga teacher, Shosha, says we are always adjusting inside the pose; the pose is all about adjusting and so is life. They are an integral muscle of the movement. If your muscles don't have space and ease, they grip and get stuck. Hello, fascia.

* Feel your body on the floor and in the room.

* Allow yourself to go to a part of your body that is hurting.

* Give it your breath and attention. Take your time here.

* Then feel your lower jaw and the relationship it has with your hips. Place your fingertips on your jaw, giving it a little loosening massage. If it feels good, you can massage your entire face. Now feel your hips. . . . What is changing?

* Feel the conversation your shoulders are having with your low back. Breathe as you stretch and circle your shoulders, up and around, forward and backward. Roll them back and feel your tailbone and what it's trying to say.

* Stretch your arms and feel into all they carry.

* Feel your low belly. . . . Let it soften. Stretch your full body like a cat—like the ones finally napping in the side room, remember?

* Feel into your solar plexus and experience the view from there.

* In feeling your way through your body, you might notice something new, something old, something you don't want to feel, something that surprises you with joy and lightness.

* You will never know until you begin.

* Make room, breathe, and take
  your time.

"Keep finding new ways to go to
    the same old places."[11]

Gabrielle Roth, Sweat Your Prayers

Your stories are in your hips, your throat, your shoulders, your heart space. Your stories are also in your wrists, your low belly, your jawbone, and ankles. Your movement practice depends on you moving. Your body knows what to do. Once you start to move, you enter the next level of you. We begin to break free of habits and limits as we move, making way for our divine selves. When you practice being "out of your mind," you can get closer to your body. Curiosity becomes a soft place to land. Add your favorite music, and you may want to stay longer. You could love it here.

You are entering the relationship of your lifetime. An unconditional relationship with your beloved body is the best gift you could ever give yourself and your legacy. As you get to know you, you understand that your body is not only an offering to the earth; it is the earth. I have no idea if you can see me, but I'm stretching with you. I am inviting you to stretch with me. Your body is amazing. Oh, what an intimate space! Oh, what an intimate life! This is where possibility lives. You are possible. You are alive!

word tinctures

take a few drops of one sentence below

place it under your tongue

let it move you

say it out loud as you move

as you walk inside your day

let it change you

I am here now.

I am not going anywhere without you.

I want to learn from you.

I want to hear you.

I see you.

I feel you.

I love you.

I am here to take care of you.

I am never leaving you again.

You are everything.

I am listening.

Thank you for being my body.

"You are how you move."[12]

Gabrielle Roth, Sweat Your Prayers

move you: making room

Okay, it's time to put on some music you really love. You can stay on the floor, you can stretch some more or you can get up and shake that booty. . . . Permission is everywhere. What does it feel like to be ready? What does it look like to be ready? Do you put on the leggings and look for the headphones? Do you wait until you feel like it? Do you tell your body that you will get to her, him, them later? What does it look like to move in the day-to-day? Why is it so much easier to call the dentist and wait on hold for an hour than to get up and move your body? The bridge to moving your body can feel long and rickety. It is like the bridge into the kitchen. This is your practice. You can move while you are on hold. You can move while you are reading this sentence. You are free to move any way you want to. Just move! Hit the play button and begin. What are you waiting for?

* If you are still on the floor, find your way to your feet.

* Begin to walk around the room at whatever pace feels good.

* Find your breath and repeat these words: "Feet to floor, floor to feet."

* Notice your rhythm, your gait, the balls of your feet, your ankles, arches, and the entire

"republic of you body," as my teacher Shosha says. Take all of you in.

* Walk like this for a few minutes, and let it gradually move you into the next thing you want to experience.

* Music that inspires you to move is key here. Make a playlist for this "move you" practice with rhythms and beats that vary

so you can move into different feelings and textures.

* If resistance is showing up, you can name it here. Let everyone inside of you know that you see it and feel it, and then move with it.

* Gabrielle Roth says to listen to the music with your whole body.

* Dance with all the resistance you're feeling.

* What shape is your resistance? How does it want to move? If your body was your only language, how would you show me what the resistance is saying to you?

It might feel deeply vulnerable to move. Most of us walk around with a head as our body. To unravel something in your hips or solar plexus on a Tuesday may not be trending yet. And as long as you're living as though everything else is more urgent, you'll wait a little longer before you move your body. What if I were to tell you that moving your body is an emergency. Your body moving is the best emergency that has ever happened to you. Once you start to move, you will feel all that wants to shift in you. Everything doesn't have to be so hard. We feel this once we begin to move. Moving right-sizes your heaviness. You are crossing the bridge to yourself.

Oh, and moving is not just for a good day, like on a summer evening with a glass of something sparkly in hand. Do it then, and do it the next morning when you feel tired. Do it all the time. Just do it.

do it every day!

Your body is your home. When you move your body, you come home to yourself. You don't have to carry the heaviness of your old ancestral stories for one more minute. When you are disconnected from Spirit or Source or Mama Earth—or from the blueberries in the plastic container or the suffocating sliced cremini mushrooms in the black Styrofoam carton—you can feel lost. In this loss, you can forget who you are. Remember what happens when you go hungry for you? You lose sight of the beauty around you and inside of you. Your body is here to heal with you. Your body, your wisdom. You know the quote "You are the one you are waiting for"? It is true. Your body loves you. Forever.

There has been so much in the way of you being with your body. I see you. When you move, you make the space to be intimate with yourself. You feel the sides of the deep chasm that has separated you from yourself coming back together. You can feel yourself mending as you step to the beat. You can invite safe and phenomenal people to hold, reflect, and support your healing. I love a team to move with, and I support you in gathering one. We will talk more about this in chapter 10. I am on your team. I am right here beside you. This is your dance party!

"Just beyond

yourself.

It's where

you need

to be.

Half a step

into

self-forgetting

and the rest

restored

by what

you'll meet."[13]

David Whyte,
The Bell and the Blackbird

move you: moving your lineage

Your body is a collaboration with all the bodies that came before you. This may seem like a simple enough concept, yet we don't usually think about our bodies in this way. You are not the first in your lineage to boil water, make a bath, turn on the fire, or dance. There's no way to know all of your collaborators, yet you can invite them to be with you at any time. They will show you the way. You can feel your lineage as you move your body. You are so many. You can ask them to hold you. You are moving what they couldn't move. So much of your story is their story. As you bow to their journey, you bow to yours.

* As you move inside the shapes of resistance or any other emotion that comes—maybe it's pain, sadness, grief, or joy—feel the freedom that is coming along for the ride. You can write it down here.

* Breathe in and out with haaaaaaaaa as you continue to feel your body move into new emotional shapes.

* Let go of what you think or how you look or, or, or . . .

* Let your body move—like, really move here! If anything is in the way of you moving, you can name it out loud as you move through it.

* Offer your mind to your feet, your breath, your beating heart, and the cats in the spare room as you bring your heartbeat up. You are moving you!

* When you are ready, you can center yourself and find your breath.

* You can say, internally or out loud, "Thank you for my life, thank you for your life."

* You can begin to picture energies of your bloodline behind you and around you.

* You can tell them, "I see your heavy fate. I no longer need to carry it moving forward. I am giving it back to you."

* Then honor them and say, "I honor you and your life. Thank you for my life."

You can offer love and respect as you free yourself of their heaviness. When you set yourself free, you set them free. You no longer need to carry the burden that they carried. Lineages of heavy fate create all kinds of disorder in our bodies. The mystery of your chronic pains, dis-ease in all the ways, and autoimmune everything, along with your beliefs, fears, and ways of living that served our ancestors may not serve you now. Maybe their fears kept our great-grandparents safe and got them through, yet that heavy burden is not for you to carry any longer.

When you feel this heaviness, you can turn on the music, find your feet, and say these words. You are able to do the good work they were not able to do. You are clearing the way for everyone who comes after you. You honor your lineage and yourself by doing this *family constellation* work. Through this healing process, you set everyone free. Moving your body makes room for this deep healing. Healing is a collective "contact" sport with the family you know and the family you will never meet. Your healing supports the entire family tree, its branches, roots, and the forest it's part of. Healing is a priceless inheritance to pass down. Healing is your legacy.

move you: slowing down to the pace of life

Your relationship with your body is one of the most intimate experiences you will have. It will invite you to have conversations with every part of you. It will bring you all the way to our first mother, Mama Earth. You were born to be the steward for this body. As you align to this way of living, being, moving, and healing, you can begin to hear your truth. You discover a compass that can guide you from the old ways of control and judgment to patience, love, and trust. You are moving toward who you truly are. You are witnessing the incessant fears and pain that kept you safe yet small. All you have to do is show up. You can't fail.

* As you move from your practice into your day, take it with you.

* Allow yourself to go slowly here.

* You can say, "There is nothing to fix about me," as you pour a glass of water.

* You can say, "I am love," as you feel your feet on the floor.

* Put your hand on your heart space and begin to loosen your front chest and back.

* There is no rush here.

* Breath in: "I am held."

* Breathe out: *Haaaaaaaaa.*

* Say out loud, "I am love!"

* Can you hear your body?

* What did your body just say? Write it here.

Finding the way to your freedom is powerful. When you carve the time out to be with your body and move what is here, you can heal the way you inhabit your life. This practice unravels your old stories and makes room for freedom. After freedom sets in, ease, permission, and beauty show up in abundance. These are the medicinal ways that grow stronger as you use them. Letting your body know that you are here, inside all of the to-do lists, nonstop needs, and heavy conditioning, is the bravest work. It is brave because it is not reflected in the mainstream . . . yet. You are pioneering this freedom in your life. Your body is the invitation to your freedom.

reclaiming your body

The language of your body is subtle, and it usually happens under the radar. Your old body story is a silent inheritance. It is passed to you through modeling and loads of sense memory. Much of our individual body stories were shaped by what the culture said, the church screamed, and science deemed—leaving little to no room to explore and discover the unique body you came into the world with. Then add your lineage stories and some bloodline goodness, and you will have yourself a heavy story to carry around. This has been your blueprint for living. The good news is that you don't actually need this blueprint ever again.

missing me

There is a loneliness that can emerge when you go hungry for yourself. When you feel disconnected from your body, you can get hungry for everyone and everything out there. It can feel sticky, leaky, and uncomfortable. You might feel heavier than usual, regardless of an actual size change, and bloated or off in one way or another. I usually feel like the pufferfish in the movie *Finding Nemo*—in any heightened situation she blows up like a balloon. I know I need to move, yet the stagnant energy of not wanting to wins. This is when I have to move. This is where your practice lives. Right here, at this corner of *Sticky Avenue* and *Inside Lane*. The practice is not in actually moving your body—it is in *connecting* to your body in this way. It is in crossing the bridge to yourself. It is in making it to the middle way. This is what support looks and feels like.

Even in reading and writing and talking about the body, it feels like we are separating ourselves from *feeling* the body. That is the risk I am taking here to share this with you. My wish is that you will set the book aside and begin to move. You are the only one who can do this for you. There is nothing to wait for. There is so much abundance in your YES. You can begin again and again and again. My wish is that you will bring your body with you everywhere you go. Your body wants to tell you what it knows. This is not information you can access from your mind. Move your body to the music you love. Pray in the kitchen while you sauté kale or rainbow chard or make a quiche. When you feel closer to you, you remember who you are. When you remember who you are, you nourish you, and everyone you love, from a full cup. As you move into the kitchen, you might find yourself healing.

"I move to remember so many things. I move to shake up all the stagnant energy held captive in the crevices of my body. I move to collect all the energy I have given away both knowingly and unknowingly. To collect all of the fractured pieces of my being and hold them in the sweet framework of my heart. I wiggle to remember what it felt like to move as a child, before I learned to care what I looked like or how someone might judge it. I move to break down the walls that keep me from deeply connecting to me."

Maggie

Rebirth

We never stop becoming.
And how exhausting it is
to regroup, to revive
and again and again
find the source of renewal.
Yet, the charge is set
just like the waves,
and in every crest,
in each deep valley,
we find reason to celebrate
being anything at all.
To know the richness
of the dark is to better
weep in the light. Find
solace in this rhythm,
for there is no other way.
Go, ask the moon if it
gets to stop its cycle.
-j.suskin
Feb 2018

thank you, body.

"Let yourself love what you love, and see if it doesn't lead you back to what you ate when you loved it."[14]

Tamar Adler, An Everlasting Meal

part 3

healing in the kitchen

cooking up a life you love

invitation

We come into the kitchen because we are hungry, not just for food but to heal our lives. So much of our lives, and our living, happens in the kitchen. We honor rituals like marriage, holidays, and reunions. We celebrate the joy of birth and grieve the sadness of death. It is in the kitchen where we are also hungry to connect, to be together and take care of each other. There is an intimacy in these moments—offering love, belonging, and all the essential ingredients to nourish our lives.

To cook up your life is to be in the daily practice of who you are becoming, which is all about food but goes beyond food too. To turn on the fire in the kitchen is to ignite your heart and the hunger it carries. We may not realize that our hunger is also an invitation to connect with ourselves. When we come into the kitchen, so much is possible inside our hunger—we want to move and be moved by each other, by the beauty of our food, our life and all it gives us. Nourishing your life is a tending to your story—the story you *want* to be living every day. Even if we don't *know* it, we can *feel* the loss of this connection if there is no cultural holding or ritual around something as essential as cooking and eating. When growing your own food, healing as a way of living, and connecting deeply with each other are luxuries you do once in a while, if ever, there is a problem. In a cultureless culture, living your becoming is a pioneer's journey.

For many of us, our childhood kitchen was a place where the old stories of perfection and obligation played out in unhealthy ways. This was the place where words like *resentment*, *I do it all*, and *I am the only one that does anything around here* lived and thrived. They were also the titles to the top hit songs of my childhood.

When you claim your kitchen as a place to BE, you offer yourself to the sacred rhythm inside a simmering kettle, a cake plate of Honeycrisp apples, a candle lit by an open bowl of salt, a block of room temperature butter, and a wood board. Your kitchen will meet you right where you are. This is the place where many of your stories were birthed. It is also the place where you can rebirth yourself. Your "essential ingredients" live inside your values, your body wisdom, and the profound spaciousness you are discovering here. Your kitchen is your mother waiting to love you.

we are all hungry

As you warm the cast-iron pan, melting salted butter and the sweet yellow onion, something softens inside. As you sauté what longs to be transformed with a wood spoon and light pink salt, you can listen for the feeling of this moment. You are taking your stories out of a brown paper bag, to be brushed clean, chopped, and added to your soup on simmer. You are healing as your feet root, grounding toward something secure and consistent, so you can attach and grow.

In this section, I am inviting you into *your* kitchen. In chapter 6, you will meet your kitchen as a place to be, a space that wants to nurture and cherish you. Your kitchen is love, abundance, and possibility. It is also a place of tending beauty inside the landscape of your values. It is a place that will hold you no matter what you bring to it. In chapter 7, you will learn about beauty as a vital ingredient to your healing and becoming. You will move into a rhythm that guides how your home feels, runs, and supports everyone in it. As you gather these ingredients for making space, you will feel a lightness that can hold you in the kitchen, with the fire and your body. As you bring these remedies into chapter 8, you will begin to establish new traditions, originating a culture of nourishing yourself and those you love. This culture is called *wood board love*. As you spend time in a kitchen you love to be in, you will feel inspired and supported to cook up your best life. You will begin to make what you love.

"Love is a place
& through this place of
love move
(with brightness of peace)
all places"[15]

E.E. Cummings

To be is to exist[16]

Being is the nature or essence of a person[17]

chapter 6

a place to be

A place to be is a place where you bring your essence. It is a place to bring all of you. When your kitchen is a place to be, nourishing your life becomes an integrative practice. Your days change from a series of stress-induced separations from yourself to invitations to get closer and rekindle your connection inside. When your main intention is *to be*, you no longer forget who you are inside what you are doing. You can read that again. Take it in. It is new for all of us. There is nothing to reach for, squeeze into, or rush toward when you are right here, awake inside your life. When what you *need to do* is folded in with *how you want to be*, your relationship with who you think you are begins to change, and a new way of living emerges. Freedom and time for you is no longer a distant fantasy—it is right here and now.

Oh yes, you are still doing all the regular daily things like making lunches, trying to figure out if the seaweed is nuclear and the string cheese is organic, preparing breakfast, thinking about dinner, doing the dishes for the millionth time. And that is just food related. What about work, kids, marriage, parents, friends, Mother Earth, and on and on? We are so consumed with the future that we rarely, if ever, make it to this moment right here. Life is in session even as you are changing within. You don't have to leave your body or the depth of you behind to go about your day. You can bring all of you with you. You can let go of the controlling ways you used to move through life in order to *get it all done*. You can also let go of the need to hide or secretly find time for yourself in the late hours of the night as you sacrifice sleep or other basic needs to support your body. You don't need any of these coping mechanisms when you bring yourself with you.

You are slowing everything down to the present moment. This is vulnerable terrain. It is the field of your feelings and actually feeling them. Over time, even your heaviest stories of heartbreak will align themselves easefully in your day. As you walk closer to your becoming, you can ring that fantasy bell in knowing that *being* is not trending yet and you are done living like a banshee!

To emerge from old ways of living and coping into a new way of being is some of the deepest work you will ever do. You will look around to discover that most people are still trapped under the eighteen-wheeler truck that is our stressed, busy, malnourished culture. You are the one getting yourself out. You are letting go of an old blueprint that doesn't work anymore. You are blazing a trail to love yourself and never leave yourself again.

What does this look like in the day-to-day? You walk away from your desk of a million things to do and go into the kitchen. You turn the oven to 375 degrees. You gather a kobocha, butternut, or red kuri squash from the center of the dining table and place it in a casserole dish. You pour some olive oil on it and slide it into the oven. You pour quinoa into the rice cooker with coconut milk and love. You warm a tea and return to your office. You are softening the hardness. You are *being* and *doing*. You are nourishing you as you host meetings, make appointments, and become the badass human you have always known yourself to be! You are getting ahead of it. You are letting the kitchen offer its medicine to you inside your day. You are right-sizing what might show up at work or with family by enveloping it in cozy aromas and vibrant flavors. Getting food into the oven with the fire, letting the cooking hold you while you work and tend to the other needs of the day nourishes that banshee inside. This is your healing practice.

Banshee: a female spirit in Gaelic folklore whose appearance and/or wailing warns a family that one of them will soon die.[18]

a place to heal

Your kitchen is a space of unconditional love. A place where you can break open, make a mess and cook up something delicious, like a life. All you need is a wood board, a knife that feels good in your hand, and food that you really love. You can transform your legacy inside the softest scrambled egg, sautéed greens, and a small scoop of apricot-honey goat cheese. You can rebirth yourself inside a variety of cakes that call for just a handful of ingredients. As you slow down to the pace of your life, the edges pull away from the pan and create a space for you to be. The aroma calls you home again and again.

Your kitchen is also a fierce mother holding what is ripe and ready to become. It doesn't take long to feel safe in here no matter what story you carry. Space is important even in the smallest of kitchens. Everybody likes their own wide wood bowl to rest in for the night. Healing in the kitchen is about timing and rhythm and yes, more tending. It is also about a kind of intuitive beingness and courage and beauty. Everything is about beauty as you stand at the island lighting the candle beside the to-do list, or gather yourself at the sink full of dirty dishes.

This is that *meditation moment* you have been waiting for as you put on some music you love, breathe, and make this moment yours. As you feel your feet on the floor, you might reclaim an old fantasy of cooking and the ample notes you took as a child, you slowly begin to surrender to a new way of being. Today, your curiosity peeks out from the silverware drawer as your willingness shows up to write a new story. You are learning that you can *be* in the kitchen as well as *do* in the kitchen. You see shame and guilt, vulnerability and grief, all having *a forever conversation* around the kitchen island. You lean in closer to hear what they have to say as you put a big heart-shaped wood board in front of them. You slice a block of mild cheddar, warm a small sourdough boule, scoop a big dollop of salted butter, add some sliced French radishes and honey dates. You cut up a happy mountain of d'Anjou pears and Gala apples near the rice crackers. You feel at ease. This is not an event. You are gathering a new language for becoming who you are in the kitchen. You are in the kitchen with freedom and permission.

You are learning about skin-to-skin contact with yourself and this deeper place inside of you. You are feeding what has been waiting for you. Truly taking care of yourself possibly for the first time. This is your kitchen healing.

quinoa in the rice cooker

It always feels good to have things working for you when you are busy working, too. Here we are at the rice cooker again. Though you don't need a rice cooker for this recipe or any recipe in this book (you can use a saucepan with a lid), what I love about it is that it can be on while you go about your day. It works *for you*. This is one of those recipes that is dear to my heart. It was in place of the mother, grandmother, and friend that I longed for as I was becoming a mother. I was home alone, immersed in naps and breastfeeding, learning how the hours of the day pass in a whole new way. I would put this mix of love together to feed myself and then, over time, to feed my babies, my friends, and now YOU! It saved me during a time when I really needed a tribe. You have a tribe in me and all the women in this gorgeous community. This recipe will support you like a tribe, and remind you that you are never alone in your kitchen and in your life.

tools

rice cooker or saucepan you love

wood spoon

linen cloth over your shoulder or nearby

a 2-cup measuring glass

gather

a little spoonful of ghee or butter

1½ cups organic quinoa

½ cup (canned) cooked organic
   garbanzo beans

½ cup frozen or fresh English peas

a handful of dried wild blueberries
   or dried cherries

1 can of organic coconut milk

1½ cups of water

you can also add frozen or fresh organic sweet potato or butternut squash

The beauty of the rice cooker is you can throw everything in and let it cook on its own. Take all the ingredients listed above and put them together in the rice cooker, maybe giving it a stir. This can feel deeply healing inside our busy lives. One tip: once you pour the coconut milk into the rice cooker or saucepan, you can fill the can with water and use that water toward the 1½ cups in the recipe (this makes sure you get all the coconut milk out of the can!). Like oatmeal, quinoa is 2-to-1, which means 2 parts liquid to 1 part dry grain. So whatever the measurement of the grain, double the liquid. Another hint: let this be in the rice cooker well after it is "done" by the rice cooker or kitchen timer. It is really good when it has had some time to settle a bit. You can make this in the morning, and by lunch, or anytime throughout the afternoon, it will get better and better. It can be in a bowl with sliced goat gouda, squash, and any protein, or on its own. It can be warmed up the next day or you can add an egg and a little flour to make quinoa patties. It is the gift that keeps giving! Enjoy, loves x x x x

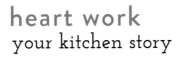

heart work
your kitchen story

As you nourish you, you begin to rewrite your kitchen story. If the kitchen was modeled as a place of drudgery, obligation, and perfection, then feeling into words like *permission, ease,* and *freedom* might be a little new for you. Listening to yourself, and the flow you want to be in, serves everyone. Your work is to tune in to where you are in the moment. Feel yourself first. Remembering you supports you in feeling your rhythm and where your body is today. We do this in the kitchen all the time. You are not looking outside yourself to see if the coast is clear or if you are safe. You are checking in on the inside first. When you tend to you first, the energy to nourish your world will sustain you, and everyone you love, with ease.

♡   Gather that journal you love, and a pen you love too. Also a timer.

♡   Find a place that is cozy and quiet. Perhaps you have made this place for yourself by now, but if not, support is on the way (in the next few pages).

♡   Turn on the timer for eleven minutes.

♡   At the top of the page, write: *The kitchen is a place where . . .* or *I find myself in the kitchen when . . .* Your kitchen story is usually a part of your other stories—like the ones about waking up in the morning—the conditions you were shaped in or your body story, just to name a few.

♡   Allow yourself to let goooooooooo here, to write like a banshee. Don't stop for anything—don't worry what it sounds like or looks like or if it is even true. You never want to get in the way of your genius!

- ♡ Give yourself time to write YOUR STORY. You can write inside this prompt for a whole week, doing it every day for seven days to see what happens.

- ♡ So much will come as you allow yourself to be free.

- ♡ You will learn things you may have never known about yourself.

- ♡ When you give yourself space in this way, the medicine rises to meet you.

The days of giving from an empty cup, half a cup, or no cup at all are coming to an end. No one is nourished when the cook is not fed, yet somehow that became the mold many of us live our lives inside—a contest of how empty you can be and still do. Bye, borrrring story! Cooking food and putting it out for others so you can go do the dishes and not eat until the scraps come back doesn't serve anyone. It actually models exactly what it is: "I take care of you, but I don't take care of myself. Taking care of you takes care of me. If you are good, I am good." Ummmm, hello, codependence on line one, two, and three, please hold. I am picturing the scene in 9 to 5 with the amazing Dolly Parton, Jane Fonda, and Lily Tomlin sitting around the coffee table laughing so hard they were crying. They were naming this in spades.

Your new story can sound more like:

> I am taking care of me and you. We can do this together. I love to nourish me while I nurture you. When I take care of me, I see and feel my life in a whole new way. I have space for all of us. I have space for possibility. I make decisions from a place of fullness. I can see what is aligned and feels good to me. When I nourish me, I can nourish you in a full, true, and deep way. We both are fed.

You don't need to burn your apron with your bra when you nourish you first. You are becoming someone who keeps the butter out and creates altars everywhere you go. All of a sudden, you are aware of how the deep valley of a wide wood spoon and that pristine spot on the tip of your tongue can become dear friends within a moment's notice. You are getting closer to who you are. You reach for a ladle and your mother's copper pot as you turn the heat on low. You are gathering Bosc pears as you harvest mint and lemon verbena from the garden in the backyard. You are making your way to healing as a way of living. This is your life.

a place that feels like you

When you walk into your kitchen, does it feel like you? Do you see things that resonate with who you are? Does it feel good, stressful, or a bit of both? Does it have the feeling of a vacant lot, an airport, a gas station, or even a morgue? Is it a shit show or a lovefest or everything in between? Or maybe your kitchen feels like a cozy cashmere womb, and it's where you spend all your time. Or your kitchen might be like a pair of khaki pants: pretty neutral and goes with everything. Maybe you have never thought about how your kitchen feels. You might be thinking, *Jules, it's just a kitchen. What's the big deal? The white plates are fine, they work.*

The thing is, your kitchen reflects your life. When you change how your kitchen feels, it can support you to change how *you* feel. This is a foundational ingredient to how you heal. When you align your kitchen to flow with ease and freedom, it supports you to flow with ease and freedom. Tending the space on the outside helps you tend the space on the inside.

I am inviting you to create a space where you are inspired to cook and move and heal and grieve and love and *be* in your kitchen. A space that embodies a world of YOU everywhere you look. Creating a space that feels like you begins with the ingredients you are gathering here on your journey. As you slow down, you might hear the footsteps of your old stories coming in. They want to tell you that *this is not the time* or *you don't have money for new things* or *you hate clutter in the kitchen.* You are not alone with the stories of clutter and scarcity and change. It's a long game, remember? These old stories are attempting to protect you. We can bow to their service, offer gratitude for them watching out for you. You can offer them a warm thyme tea for their inevitable grief and some wood board love to enjoy. As you name what might be coming up for you, you can get closer to hearing the truth inside of you. This is one of the greatest steps toward your growth. Feed what is hungry with what you love. Name what is here and bring it to the light. You are tapping into the voice you might have heard during a long drive; a warm, life-giving shower; or a walk in the forest. This is your intuition. You are not broken, and neither is your hunger. Changing a pattern is quiet and powerful work. I see you healing.

hello, body!

feeling you in the kitchen

* When you walk into your kitchen, do you see you? Do you feel you? Is the space cluttered with things that feel like other people live here? Like the gifts held onto out of guilt, something from a friend that really doesn't feel like you, homemade clay figures from your kids that you love and could maybe go somewhere else, or an appliance that matches the color palette but, again, just doesn't feel like you . . .

* You are going to make a space that feels like you. We'll start by clearing a wide area on the kitchen island or dining room table, moving aside all the clutter and stuff that occupy this space.

* Gather all the things you have never loved or resonated with . . . it is here that you can let go of the stories that don't align with your journey and make space

for the ones that do. Let this be a healing process.

* It is important to take this one moment, one inch, one plate or bowl or object at a time—there's no need for an all-or-nothing approach here. We are taking our time and letting powerful change happen gradually.

* You are not hurting anyone by loving what you love. If you share the space with your partner or a roommate, this is a GORGEOUS opportunity to have a healing conversation about how this space can be tended, sharing what you want and hearing what they want, too.

* Whenever you find yourself in a temporary kitchen situation, you can always make something, even a little area, feel like you. This could happen with a basket or bowl you love for the tea or fruit.

* As you feel into your body and this newly opened space, what feels like love to you?

* Take your time here; it is so special and sacred to create spaces that reflect who you are. Let something sit for a day or two and see if it feels like you. If not, let it go.

* Getting to know what you love, and letting the spaces you occupy reflect that, is healing work.

Being in a kitchen that feels like you inspires you to cook delicious food AND live a life you love. Perhaps you cook all the time, but you find it stressful. Maybe you love to cook, but you just can't find the time. Or perhaps your story is that you love your kitchen, but you are never home. Or that you love to cook, but you are having a dry spell inside a big life transition. Or maybe you won't go anywhere near the kitchen since that space is for someone else. Whether you identify with something here or a different story, your kitchen will always meet you right where you are. You can write your story right here in the margin. You can witness it shifting as you gather and grow here.

gather what you love

As a child, you might have seen your grandmother's fancy plates, silver, or fine china kept behind a glass hutch, only to be used for holidays or special occasions. Maybe you inherited a few pieces or the whole set, and it is collecting dust in the garage. You don't know what to do with it. This is another place where you can gather what you love and let go of what you don't. Are you waiting for a special occasion? Do you want that fancy feeling inside your day-to-day? Perhaps you want to use the crystal bowls for cereal and milk in the mornings. Why not? And what are you waiting for? I love a fancy moment to break open the old conditioning of what a cereal bowl should look and—even better—feel like! Or maybe you never liked them, and they bring up guilt and confusion for you every time you see them. They are expensive heirlooms, yet they don't feel like you or align with your lifestyle now. Are you ready to set yourself and the fine china free? Will you allow yourself to change the story? You probably know someone who would love this fancy set of floral porcelain goodness. As you get closer to you, you will feel clear on what you want to do. The inquiry of *what you love* asks the question *Who am I?* Actually, everything on this healing journey asks the question *Who am I? Who am I* to give away these special heirlooms from my family? And *who am I* to keep these in storage and not use them until my kids have their own homes and will pay for more storage to keep what they never saw out? *Who am I* to give them away to someone who will love and adore them so I can make space in my life for what I love and adore?

Slowing down is the answer to everything.

When you see something you love in a store, what happens? Do you rush toward it or wait, trying to locate the price tag before you let yourself touch it? Do you dream about it for days but never go back to get it? What is your story of seeing something that feels like you and then gathering it for you? Other places where your stuck stories could be living are possibly in the garage. Have you unpacked the Cuisinart from the wedding gifts? It might feel like it's just too much, which can lead to getting stuck, overwhelmed, or paralyzed inside your life. Hi. I get it.

There are so many ways you can gather what you love in your kitchen. Your home is already a wonderful store for vessels and items you may never have imagined could go in the kitchen. So is your basement, garden shed, or even your kid's room. There might be things in your kitchen that really don't belong there. This is where the kitchen healing begins! Perhaps the plates you eat on everyday are not plates you love. They might carry a story. They are from your ex-husband's mother, who was never kind to you. You are about to tell me, "Jules, they are just plates." I know—I can hear you from a million miles away. I am on your team here. Haaaaaaaaa . . . let's breathe together. Guess what I am going to tell you? They are not *just plates.* And they will never be *just plates.* They are the holders for the food you gathered, possibly grew, and transformed to nourish you. Even if you are eating a hotdog and fries, loving the plates that hold your food supports you in creating a place you love.

Dish towels are another area where we often don't consider what we truly love. The kitchen is not a bathroom! And having terrycloth black towels has never inspired anyone, especially when you can gather beauty in their place. Perhaps you love linen and the way they soften over time, but you never let yourself buy them.

Or you avoid flour-sack towels because they stain. Let them stain! Let them soften! Let goooooooooo into loving what you love and see who you become.

If you are new at gathering things you love, take your time. It is really such a joy to let go of all the stuff that has been in the way. The old stories about *what you deserve* and *what you are worth* can go have a double scoop of cookie dough ice cream as you clear away what doesn't feel like you. Sit with this feeling before you move on to something else. As you feel more and more permission here, you might find your pace increasing until all of a sudden you are zooming around as though the house is on fire. I know—I do it too. I am inviting you to feel into your freedom here and really slow down to feel the care and love you are giving to yourself. You are tending your reawakened fire.

The intention here is to love everything you see, hold, and use to mix, cut, pour, stir, sift, boil, and sieve. This is where your essence lives. It is time to offer those plates to someone who doesn't have a story associated with them. There are people you know who need those plates. Free yourself from all the things you don't love and make room for the things you do. Places, objects, and stories hold energy. If the energy doesn't feel like you, it will stop the flow of everything. If you want a loving, easeful flow in the kitchen, you need to make the space for the flow, to, well, *flow*. Finding your flow is part of your healing.

You might have a pot from Spain that was intended for a plant, but you notice it's actually a fantastic holder for your wood spoons. You might have been using a wood board as a centerpiece on your living room table. Bring it into the kitchen, to the left of your stovetop, as a spot for your olive oil, salt bowl, and wide clay bowl of onions, garlic, and alliums. You don't need a lot; you only need what you love. And guess what happens? You begin to cook with love! You *create* love! You live a life of love when everywhere you look you see your love.

I have never met a basket, a wood spoon, or a French glass jar that I didn't love. I can't seem to get enough soft linens, as they are useful in many realms—napkins, kitchen towels, table dressings, aprons, the list goes on. If we are ever in a store together, you will find me by the little ceramic pinch pots that hold olive pits, strawberry tops, tangerine piths, and more. I love all the beautiful things that can hold for us. Let them hold for you as you become you.

altars everywhere

When you walk into a working home kitchen, it is warm and loving, worn and stained. It is devoted to all that is stirring and rising and transforming. It feels like a soft place to land. There is a consistent flow of care that keeps the house warm, regulated, and nourished. If you long for your kitchen to feel like this, you are on your way. You don't have to wait to create spaces that remind you of who you are. Wherever you are, geographically or in your life, you can make sacred and intentional areas called altars.

You have gathered things you love. You are making room to be seen. You are opening to freedom inside yourself. You are moving the loud packaging to the side. You are bringing in the glass Ball jars so you can see your food. You are removing the berries from the plastic container and placing them in open bowls in the fridge. You are setting everything free. You are setting yourself free.

You are giving your food a place to *be*. You are making sure everyone can see what they need. You are creating altars everywhere.

heart work
altars everywhere

Everything can be an altar. Your books, your pantry, even your toilet paper and how you stack it in the cabinet can all be areas for altars. Altars alter how we see our things, and our lives. In putting your tools out with intention, you set yourself up to live, cook, and heal in a creative way. Remember, you are bringing all of you—to the oven, the island, and to the altars that hold you.

Stand at your kitchen sink. Is there a window sill or a space there in front of you? What do you see? What do you *want* to see? If your view is of the next building, a house or a wall, you can create something you prefer to see. Is there a sill nearby or an area where you can set out a few things you love? If yes, begin with placing that piece of paper with the name of your journey here. You can use art tape as it is colorful and doesn't hurt the walls or windows.

A handmade bowl or little clay container here can remind you that you are held here. This can be a special spot for a stone, gem, or shell you gathered on one of your walks or travels. This can also be a place to put your rings or any jewelry while cooking or doing the dishes.

Bring in the earth. Perhaps some rosemary or basil from the garden in a Ball jar with a bit of water to nourish it. You will be inspired to use this with your cooking, too. You can buy yourself some gorgeous flowers from the local flower shop and put a few here. Why are you buying the flowers? Because you are alive and healing and breathing into your becoming!

You can place your beeswax candle here. Depending on the room, it could be a thin candle, votive, or pillar you light as you make the ordinary extraordinary.

Altars can hold what is hungry to change, what needs healing. You can bring your daily altar offerings. Creating altars transforms your kitchen from *a place of meh* to a *loving space of haaaaaaaaa.*

buy the flowers.
warm the tea.
gather beauty.

beauty heals

In the early kitchen healer days, one of the first things I would do upon entering a new client's home was go on a little scavenger hunt. I was on the lookout for a clear vessel. A Ball jar, glass pitcher, or any kind of heavy, transparent carafe. Once I found it, I would scan the counters, fruit bowls, fridge, or garden for anything citrus. Usually, I would find a super wrinkled lime or lemon hiding in the corner of a hanging basket under some atrophying garlic and some old bread bag ties. This was also where I might find the client's shame and vulnerability.

As I brought the barely breathing lime to the cutting board, I would begin to resuscitate it. First, I would take the sticker off of its faded green skin and slice it open. I would put a few "bicycle wheel" slices in the glass vessel as I continued on my search for herbs—mint, basil, rosemary, thyme, whatever I could find. I might come across some bone-dry oregano inside a half-open plastic container (the ones you can never close once you open them—you know the ones!) near the butter, or maybe some browning mint in the drawer with the deli meats. If I was lucky, I would find something growing in the garden. I would cut it close to the root, harvest a little bouquet, and bring it inside. I might put a few stems in a tiny vase to place at the center of the table or near the sink as an offering. The other herbs would go in the vessel with the lime and perhaps a few slices of hothouse cucumbers I might have found during my hunt.

As my client would make her way into the kitchen, she would find me pouring water into this glass vessel of foraged herbs, citrus, and cucumber with a few small glasses next to it. This was an offering for our time together. The beauty would hold us and ground our beginning. This would bring my client delight and excitement, to see her "things" she didn't even know she had used in this new way. The expression on her face would be one of amazement with a side of "Wait, I can do that!"

This was not brain surgery, yet beauty does invite us to change the chemistry inside our brains, drawing us closer to our hearts. And as you know by now, this offering wasn't just about *what I did*. If we made this about doing, it would be just another thing on the to-do list. There was something deeper than "doing" happening. Yes, I was nourishing our time together with beauty and goodness, *and* I was getting ahead of it. I was looking for, and listening to, what was in the way of this kitchen being a place of supportive ease, inspiring freedom and unconditional love. I was drawing a bridge from

what they had available into what was possible in the moment.

This is foundational. It requires changing your mind, which guides the rhythm to shift toward holding what you value. Harvesting herbs in your backyard, or even planting them in the first place, takes time. Even though it may start out as topical, or a "fake it till you make it" kind of feeling, showing up for yourself can and will integrate into a practice. Offering yourself time to value what you love and giving yourself this experience on a regular weekday is another essential ingredient to becoming you. You are navigating how this makes you feel on the inside, not just performing it because it looks good on the outside. You have all that you need around you. The key is inside the pause as we turn on the fire, feel our feet, and tend to what we love. This is your invitation to beauty.

When the food you gather and the way you care for it becomes a priority, you set yourself up to nourish your remembering. When you show up for beauty, it offers you what you may not be able to see in yourself—yet. As I searched my client's kitchen for a clear vessel, citrus, and herbs, I was creating an offering to initiate a beginning. I was making beauty to ground and move us. Beauty calls us into the kitchen, and into our best lives. This isn't complicated here on the page; yet in our conditioned, busy, nonstop days, it can feel challenging and impossible. Beauty creates space in our minds and bodies that we can't seem to find our way to in the clutter and chaos of our days. But when we move through our resistance, we discover deep healing on the other side.

the story of our lives * happens in the kitchen — it evolves over time —

"Beauty is startling. She wears a gold shawl in the summer and sells seven kinds of honey at the flea market. She is young and old at once, my daughter and my grandmother. In school she excelled in mathematics and poetry. Beauty doesn't anger easily, but she was annoyed with the journalist who kept asking her about her favorites—as if she could have one favorite color or one favorite flower. She does not mind questions though, and she is fond of riddles. Beauty will dance with anyone who is brave enough to ask her."[19]

J. Ruth Gendler,
The Book of Qualities

beauty water

This beauty water is one thing you don't have to go to the spa for. I mean, what are you waiting for? Having this in the fridge, on the kitchen island, or in the center of the dining room table says: "Hello! Come sit and enjoy this moment of your life." Oh, and we need so much more water than we are currently drinking, so here is a gorgeous invitation to drink more water with beauty!

tools

glass pitcher, carafe, or vessel you love

a long wood spoon

knife

wood board

open bowl or compost bucket

Ball jars or glasses

gather

any herbs, citrus, and veggies you can find that you would love to put in water!

You know the way to your own beauty water. One thing that will support you in creating this is making it accessible—have your citrus in a bowl near the knives and a board. Like the tea area, this is an active altar to something you love to make. This will inspire you to make it more than once. Enjoy, loves x x x x

the vital need for beauty

To know beauty as a vital need is to understand beauty as a medicine way. To under-stand the way of beauty is to let it move you into the possibility of change and limitless loving. Beauty is a space for you to receive and deepen your living right here, right now.

Beauty is an invitation that is always here. Recognizing beauty inside a non-stop, faster-better-more culture takes courage. It requires slowing down. I know, shocker. Only then do you notice the lavender rose blooming on your walk; the bees suckling honey from the sticky center of the sunflower; or how slicing the lightest, creamiest green zucchini into a sweet sauté of onion, car-rots, some nutmeg, and a bit of mint brings you straight into your life. Beauty inspires you to begin again. To stop your day, reschedule the meeting in order to go harvest the ripe and ready herbs, avocadoes or heirloom tomatoes on a weekday. Beauty is the hero's journey. *What are you waiting for?*

Please don't wait one more minute to find some beauty and bring it as close to you as you can. How are you and your body any different than the heirloom toma-to? Or the Italian fig with that particular hue of fuchsia? The chronic dis-ease and stress you carry is connected to separating ourselves from beauty. Find beauty every day, and see how differently you move in the world. Let beauty open you to the flow of your life. Gather beauty and let it mend you.

"Where beauty is, I think, is—beauty isn't all about just nice loveliness, like. Beauty is about more rounded, substantial becoming. And I think, when we cross a new threshold, that if we cross worthily, what we do is we heal the patterns of repetition that were in us that had us caught somewhere. And in our crossing, then, we cross onto new ground, where we just don't repeat what we've been through in the last place we were. So I think beauty, in that sense, is about an emerging fullness, a greater sense of grace and elegance, a deeper sense of depth, and also a kind of homecoming for the enriched memory of your unfolding life."[20]

John O'Donohue

hello, body!

all the ways beauty heals

Look for beauty.

Open your eyes.

Look to the left.

Look to the right.

What do you see?

Open your ears.

What do you hear?

Open your nose.

What do you smell?

Beauty is everywhere.

When you find beauty,

You will experience it
everywhere.

This is your practice: seeing
beauty.

You are becoming your own
healer.

Bring beauty inside with you.

Have it around you always.

When you love your life, no
matter what it brings you

You will become free.

beauty as an offering

When you surround yourself with beauty, a profound shift happens. It is not an event. To gather flowers, make an altar, tend to your food, and serve it to yourself and others is to be with beauty as an offering. An offering to gratitude, to the Earth, to wisdom, to your life. The tobacco in the fire or the roses by a headstone are daily acts of offering something over to beauty and to healing. Why are you waiting to buy the flowers? Why is it easier to buy flowers for those who have died or are sick? Offer flowers to your life and feel the beauty holding you.

Here is a little story about beauty. It was a weekday afternoon, and I was on my way to pick up my daughter, who is named Beauty, from school. It was an emotional time that had me alive with sadness, overwhelm, and fear. As we were on our way home, we were near one of the prettiest flower shops in town. Something inside me said, "Go, go to the flower shop . . . NOW!" I took a right on Green Street and found myself parking in the underground garage. Beauty asked, "What are we doing, Mommy?" I replied, "We are going to gather beauty for my heart and yours too."

We walked into the shop, and a very kind man behind the desk asked, "What are you looking for?" I said, "Beauty." He lead me to a special back area. He said, "Pick what you love and then I will arrange it for you." Then he asked, "What's the occasion?" I said, "It is for my heart." He stopped and looked up at me with

surprise. He was touched. I said, "Your love is also a part of my healing." I could see his face soften. This was becoming a healing for all of us.

Beauty and I went to the special back room, which was like an enormous refrigerator, to gather and forage from the flower-filled containers. Baby blue hydrangeas, light pink roses, hot pink dahlias, and a few other miracle flowers created this heart remedy for the day. The man and I hugged. Beauty and I went home and found a vessel for this medicine, and we put it on the table. This was an offering to the pain moving through me, which was already beginning to shift by naming it and taking care. When you listen to your heart mind, every part of your story becomes an offering to your healing.

beauty as a healer

Beauty invites you to love your life. What is winning over loving your life? What is in the way? Are you waiting for something or someone? In a culture that doesn't value beauty, it is easy to forget that beauty is a healer. When you call in beauty as your healer, it will hold your hand as you make your way to yourself. Beauty transforms the energy of a room. Arranging a vessel of zinnias or emptying a plastic container of cherries into an open bowl you love paves a path to yourself. No matter what kind of kitchen you have, you can make it yours with beauty. Beauty will always bring you home.

As beauty guides you, you might find yourself slowly and gradually cleaning out the pantry. Grains, pastas and snacks find their way into clear glass French terrines to store and see your food. This might feel like organizing, yet what you are really creating here is a place to be inspired, supported, and held. As you transform your space, you make your way to you. With beauty as your healer, you are inside an intuitive flow. You can set up little areas that reinforce your way to you. Place an essential oil near an open vessel of taper candles near a small candle holder and matches. As you light the candle, you can take a minute to apply some lavender oil onto your chest to support you. Put what you love and need in specific places to help you remember your healing. When you can see these remedies, you will use them. You are setting yourself up in the best way.

"For the experience of beauty to be strong and true, we need to be, first of all, free in our judgement. And by deepening our familiarity with beauty, we are coming in contact precisely with ourselves. We are becoming more authentic, stronger and more secure. To trust our own aesthetic judgement means to have self-esteem: We learn to be at ease with ourselves, in touch with our emotions and sensations, courageous enough to say what we feel and think. Beauty is the way we belong to the world. It is the way back to yourself. It opens your mind, gives you hope and strengthens your connection to your life."[21]

Piero Ferrucci, Beauty and the Soul

rhythm

is movement, marked by the natural
flow of related elements.[22]

tending

is to apply oneself to the care of; to
take care, to serve.[23]

heart work
the rhythm of tending beauty

I love the archaic definition of tending: *to tend is to listen.* The rhythm of tending is a listening to your natural flow. And when you are inside of your own flow, you set yourself up for *being.* As you try *being* on, you will experience that it can be woven into the *doing. Doing* and *being* become allies for your life. Again, you bring yourself with you. One of the basic ways of tending in the kitchen is to see how your food is doing, what loves to hang out together, what does not support each other, and what needed to go in the fridge yesterday. All of this guides you to what you will want to cook. How you store food, offer food, and care for your food are all inside this rhythm of listening.

When you gather food and bring it home, how do you store it? Where do you put it? How do you feel about it? Do you put things in the fridge? Do you keep things out in the package they came in? Do you put everything together in one bowl? We usually do what was modeled. And if we didn't see it modeled, many of us guess and go from there. In the guessing, grief or shame may come up. There is an emotional piece of *not knowing the basics* here, which can affect and trigger sadness. This not knowing can also bring up vulnerability around your ability to take care of yourself in the most basic ways—even if they were not taught to you. When you know the basics, you feel empowered in nourishing your foundation. Here are some everyday tips to inspire and support you!

♡ Fruit likes to hang out with each other, but from a distance. Everything has its place and, like us, most things need space to breathe. Placing different fruits and veggies in their own bowls, on cake plates, or on wood boards helps them to stay ripe longer or ripen at their own pace, without influence from others. And like us, things go smoother when everyone is in their own lane. Like prefers like, and there is an aesthetic that flows better with that, too.

♡ Onions, garlic, shallots, and all alliums love to hang out together. They are all from the same place, and they have a similar focus in life. They really *get* each other as they are fundamental to so many recipes, especially as the bases of soups, stews, and sautés. You can place them in a bowl you love next to the stovetop, and one wood board that is just for them. Having a board exclusively for onions and garlic can do wonders to keep the peace—in a marriage and in the kitchen!

♡ Avocados and bananas have the fastest of love affairs. If they sit in a bowl or on a plate together, they ripen super fast. Avocados need their own wood bowl or plate so they can have as long a life as they can get. Bananas need this kind of space, too. You can take the stickers off of everything to make them yours.

♡ Open up those netted bags and free the tangerines! You can put all your citrus— oranges, lemons, limes, and tangerines—together on a big wood board at the center of the table. This can be a beauty offering for the season.

♡ Potatoes, sweet potatoes, and other root veggies like to be more hidden from view. I love having everything out so I can see what I have, which guides what I will cook. Potatoes can turn fast, so they must be in the darkest of places or cooked immediately. I keep them out in a basket covered in linens so I don't forget about them. Other root veggies like parsnips, carrots, and beets go in the fridge, in a clear bag or drawer, again where you can see them.

♡ You want to check in with your fruit daily, or at least every other day. Move it around. When fruit is too close together or touching for too long, things get soft. Sound familiar? Offer up those plastic containers of cucumbers and berries to the farmers that need them, a local art studio, or a preschool. Hanging baskets can keep food a secret, especially if they are hard to reach.

Placing food where you can see it supports you in so many ways. The food you can see is the food you will cook!

♡   Create areas for cutting up seasonal food on a wood board. Keeping berries in a wide, low bowl in the fridge allows you to notice them and put them out on the island before a meal or as a snack. Put them in a place where kids can get to them, too! Kids love to feel empowered, just like us.

♡   Tending creates flow. Cleaning the flower water and cutting the stems, then moving the bouquet into smaller Ball jars with what is still thriving can feel good in your practice of *being* and *doing*. As you tend, you are connecting to yourself. How you put the food out, clean the fridge, and make sure everything has had some attention is a part of you nourishing you. Tending is foundational to healing. When you know what you have, you will know what to cook or bake soon. You are no longer separating from yourself. You are getting closer to what you want to create in your life and for dinner.

♡   When you are in the dark, it is easy to get lost. I mean, what *is* for dinner? Waiting for someone else to figure it out can be heavy to carry and comes with expectations and land mines you no longer need to spend time in. You can take care of you, which takes care of more than you could have ever imagined.

♡   As you make your rounds, you may feel the soft, juicy ripeness of the white nectarines. You know what will be on the pancakes tomorrow morning, or perhaps you're inspired to make a crumble of some sort. Maybe, during a week when you are too busy to bake, the nectarines go to the neighbor who loves to make morning muffins. If you miss the window, they can go to the compost or feed the chickens. No more shame spirals of wasting here. You are connected to your life now. You are becoming.

♡   You might check the Bosc and d'Anjou pears; if they feel like they have a day left, you might bake them at 350 for another nourishing lovefest with butter and a cinnamon stick or two. Baking fruit is simple, and supports the nervous system with warmth and sweetness. You can add baked pears to rice, oatmeal, a buttermilk bread, ice cream, or just pour some whole, raw cream on top and call it a day.

♡   In the doing, you can initiate a sacred time for being. You can light the candle. Put on music you love, even if it means using earphones while your babies are sleeping or if you live with someone who needs quiet. You can sing and hum and feel your feet on the floor. As you wash the dishes, you can thank them for holding what nourishes you. You are leaning into an intimate way of being.

Who knew that gathering food and bringing it into the kitchen could be a ritual of tending beauty and healing? All of a sudden, turning on the fire feels easeful and insulates this new and robust joy you are cultivating. The kitchen is becoming a place you love. So are you! You are becoming a place you love! Cooking a meal, baking a crumble, or making a wood board love is fun and full of inspiration. Your life is delicious. You have nothing to hide and everything to share.

seasonal crumble

letting the light come through as you strengthen your foundation

A crumble is so many things. It is the messy sweetness of what our lives move us into. This crumble shows us that no matter what is happening, *every little thing is gonna be alright*. I love making crumble in every season. It is a beautiful gift to bring to someone, and it takes 30 minutes, tops, to make. The aroma is inviting, and everyone who smells it wants to stay. You can make crumble for topping a pie or on its own in any deep dish you love. You can make it for twenty people or two. And my favorite part is that a crumble is also a multifaceted meal. You can have it for brekkie, snack, dinner, or dessert. This is how life can taste when it is crumbling all over the place. What a gorgeous way to nourish as the light is trying to make its way toward you. You can start with the oven on bake at 350 degrees.

tools

casserole dish or pie plate

a wide mixing bowl you love

wood spoon, hand mixer,

    KitchenAid, or the Cuisinart

linen towel

a big serving spoon you love

*you can also make this with a mix of flour
  and oats

gather

1 stick (½ cup) cold butter

3-ish cups seasonal fruit you love;

    frozen berries work too

¼–½ cup sugar (cane, maple, coconut, brown)

¾ cup gluten-free flour (or

    any kind you prefer)*

¼ tsp ground cinnamon

¼ tsp salt if the butter is not salted

whole cream if you want to make the

    whipped cream love

Bring all of your ingredients onto the counter. Start with buttering the casserole dish or pie plate, and then put your fruit in. If you are using berries and they need a little sugar and lemon—go for it. You can also thaw out frozen berries if that is the way you are headed. Depending on the season, this can be an autumn pear/apple lovefest or a summer (or anytime) berry crumble. You can bring in the spring with stone fruits—peach, nectarine, or apricot yumminess.

Gather a mixing bowl you love to put the cold butter and sugar together. Add the flour, cinnamon, and salt (if needed). Mix it all together to make the crumble topping. You can do this with a wood spoon, a hand mixer, a KitchenAid, or the Cuisinart. Use your fingers to place the crumble on top of the fruit. You can put your pie plate on a baking sheet or put it in on its own. It will cook for 30–40 minutes depending on your oven. You will know it is done when you see the juice oozing out from the brown, crisp crumble topping.

Bring it out to cool for a few minutes before serving. You can add some whipped cream or vanilla ice cream, or just straight-up cream! I mean, sky's the limit when everything is crumbling. In other words, allow this to invite you to build a newly nourished foundation. You can always warm this up for later, too. It is so good the next day. Enjoy, loves x x x x

wood board love

Ahhhhhh, welcome to wood board love! Wood board love (WBL) is a way to prepare and offer food that is ready to eat in an easeful, joyous, and FUN way! Wood board love is seasonal food sliced, diced, layered, and shared on a wood board for anyone who is hungry, which usually means everybody. And by *wood board*, I mean a board made of wood that is not stained, tinted, or tinged with toxin. That's it? Yes, that's it.

And . . . it is a life changer.

Wood board love encourages a rhythm for nourishing you and your family at any time of the day or night. It entails everything we have touched upon in your journey here—permission and freedom, beauty, healing, and holding you in that intuitive, non-eventful way that inspires you to stay in your body and *get ahead of it* at the same time. Wood board love is the daily culture of feeding you and those you love with ease in the kitchen, and in your life.

In this chapter I will share all the ways wood board love can sustain the hunger of the house before it strikes in its full splendor. As you create a place to be and allow beauty to be your healer, you will find yourself ready to make your first or five-hundredth wood board love. If you have not known yourself to be a cook (yet), this is the bridge to cooking food by gathering for the board and making food ready to eat with beauty and abundance. Such a deep and layered part of nourishing our lives is the energy in our homes and bodies around mealtimes. WBL is the daily, or hourly, remedy for that connection to remain open, light, and full of ease.

In getting ahead of the hunger we don't even know we have, we can create a rhythm for eating that is light and effortless, deep and meaningful in the flow of the day.

Wood board love invites you to eat fresh, beauty-infused, locally grown food that is cut up and ready to eat. This can also be a forever rewriting of your story in the kitchen. In showing up to the wood board, you can feel empowered and grounded in making and preparing food that is deeply healing. Offering wood board love regulates the family's nervous system, which tends to regulate yours, too! It models another way of *being and doing*. Whether you are making another wood board love or you come home to one made for you on the dining room table, you are receiving food made with love.

All you need is a wood board, a bread knife, and food you love.

the morning

By now, you have a sense of what a nourished morning can look and feel like. As you wait for the water to boil, lighting your candle on the island or the kitchen altar, you can feel your feet on the floor. You are slow and it is early, or you are fast and it is later than you want it to be—either way, you stretch and take a few haaaaaaaaa breaths. You have everything you need right here. You reach for your board. As you see your food in bowls and on cake plates and boards, you are inspired. You are not asking anyone if they are hungry. You are not asking what they want to eat. You are breathing in and out. You are creating what you love with what you have. Perhaps you are adding what they love, too. You are rewriting the story of *sacrificing in the kitchen* as you nourish YOU to feed them. You are feeling your superpowers of freedom, ease, and permission. You are making beauty.

As you reach for the strawberries, you slice the tops and cut the berries in half; you see their profound, intricate center. You slice a banana, a peach, or an apple, depending on the season, placing a handful of salted cashews down, adding a few slices of ginger or olive oil cake. You are creating a world of beauty no matter what you do. When your child, friend, or partner wakes up, they will see the candle lit and a wood board love waiting for them. This is such a gift to wake up to. This offering encompasses so much more than food. You are writing a morning story that says: "I love you. I love us. You are safe and held here. I am safe and held here."

This is what nourishing feels like. There is nothing to do or fix. You are getting ahead of it. This is not an event that calls for angst and stress. Life is in session, and this is an everyday practice. No matter what is happening, you can find your breath and be with yourself. You are free.

morning wood board love

Welcome to your first board of the day! This offering is about simplicity and joy. I am on repeat with these words because they are here for you at all times. This is about putting food out before anyone gets up or has a chance to say, "I'm hungry!" This is the comma, the pause, the moment you need to warm your tea, take a shower, make brekkie, and so on. What's on this board will shift depending on who you're preparing it for and what is in season. Don't wait for them to wake up. Get ahead of it.

tools

wood board

bread knife

open bowl, compost bucket, or bunny
  bowl for peels, tops, and cores

linen towel

gather

seasonal fruit or berries

nuts

seeds

muffins

breads

It can be easy to fill this board with sweet and sugary goodness, as it's the morning, and it can feel like a treat or party, yet this board can be FULL of nutrients and serve as a healthy breakfast or a before-brunch vibe, too. This is where you might rewrite the idea that "easy" and "fun" means "sugary" and "processed"—foods that are really good for you, like fruits, nuts, and cake, can be easy and fun, too. There's nothing "special occasion" about these foods. Yet the board and how you create it will be sacred no matter what you do. This is for every day. This is about consistency and showing up before the hunger—yours and theirs. When you start gathering for the board, your shopping list will change. Actually, you won't need a list ever again! Woot woot! As you gather seasonally, you can feel a deeper connection with your body and the earth. This will guide you into a day that is loving, light, and nourished.

the day

Whether you cook or not, wood board love is *the middle way* to making nourishing, beautiful food happen in the day-to-day. Wood board love works as a meal and between your meals. It is food for *all the time.* Integrating wood board love into your day is not a special occasion or once-in-a-while idea. It is a practice. You are gathering many practices here on your journey. It is also a ritual. Showing up with consistency (not the gripping kind) will support you in every way. When the board is kept in a place where you can't help but see it, you will use it. In the same way, placing your fresh fruit and vegetables where you can see them, in wide bowls on the counter and in the front of the fridge, will inspire you to make wood board love. Taking everything out of hiding so you can see what you have changes the landscape of eating. Everything is open; you no longer need to hide, compartmentalize, or be in the unknown. You are setting yourself up to remember, to see all you have. When nourishing your life

is everywhere you look, you begin to live this way with ease.

The full yet spacious fridge, the glass jars in the pantry, the open areas for candles, napkins, and books will heal any divide inside of you. The kitchen is your journey toward yourself. When you move the blueberries from a loudly branded container to an open bowl you love, this shifts how you feel inside. Your pantry can also be a source of inspiration when you take crackers, pastas, and dry grains out of noisy packaging and put them in glass jars. This supports seeing what you have and knowing what you will need when you go to the store. It also inspires how you want to nourish and what you actually want to put in your body. All of this sets you up to feel held in the kitchen. It sets you up to feed yourself with love.

When you begin to arrange your kitchen in service to making wood board love, it becomes a lifestyle. When in doubt, make a wood board love. When bringing food to a party, bring a wood board love. When you are not sure what's for dinner: wood board love. WBL can get food out for the family while you figure out what to do next—or it becomes dinner. Hunger doesn't wait. I can feel you nodding your head in agreement! The house can become a ravenous den of dysregulated tigers in minutes. It doesn't matter how close to dinner it is—put a wood board out! Save your life and everyone else's! You don't have to wait when it comes to wood board love. Rewrite the old story that says you can't eat before dinner. If you put what you value on the board, you will feel better. You can't fail.

It can be a snack between breakfast and lunch or lunch and dinner, or it can be an actual lunch, or an at-your-desk-nourishing-you-as-you-work-through-lunch kind of lunch. It can be an after-school pickup, board-on-the-lap-in-the-car moment, or it can be at home as the playdate arrives. It can be an afternoon tea date with a friend or a pre-dinner moment on the island. It can also be a whole afternoon-into-evening lovefest, filling the board every hour or so with goat gouda and Gala apples, Bosc pears, Castelvetrano olives and almonds, a variety of cheeses with honey drizzled on top, rice crackers, veggie chips, guacamole and salsa, roasted carrots, turnips, and cauliflower. Watermelon radishes with salted butter, cucumber spears with pink salt and olive oil, and on and on.

Put the board out while you cook. You can offer samples of what you are cooking on the board, too. Wood board love brings everyone together. It also supports any anxiety that might be coming up before dinner. Some weekdays you might get home late and it is really dinner time. This is where I can meet some pretty fierce angst. I had a busy day, I didn't get ahead of it and my kids are hungry. Nothing is in the slow cooker or warm or cooked or ready. This is the PERFECT time for wood board love. It supports my body and theirs too. I get the bath running, I light a candle, I cut up some food, get some music on, all to support me and them. This rewrites the story of anxiety around food and hunger regardless of what is actually for dinner. As you intentionally create this flow with your family, everyone is regulated and can connect while dinner cooks or is on its way from your favorite takeout. There is no more waiting for dinner. As wood board love becomes a regular happening in your home, you begin to embody the medicine that it brings. You will experience togetherness and feel the freedom of mealtimes as it creates bridges to permission every-where. You might already be doing this, as you love gathering people together, or you come from a culture of being in the kitchen together. When we make wood board love part of our day-to-day, we are fed in the deepest of ways.

daytime wood board love

The tools and process here will be similar to the morning board. The main ingredient is remembering to feed yourself in the day. We can get so caught up with meetings and clients and laundry and to-do lists that we forget to fuel ourselves. This is such a simple way to keep you and your family fed and regulated throughout the day. You can cut food up as you are on a call or even in a meeting. Fuji or Honeycrisp apple with sliced mild cheddar is pretty popular over here for a midday snack. The most popular wood board love is the one after school. No matter how old you are, everyone loves a wood board to come home to. It's fun for kids to come home and see food on the table—actually, I think that works for all of us. I've found the board is best with food in bite-size pieces. When you leave things whole, like fruit in a bowl or strawberries with their tops on, they seem to stay untouched. Freshly sliced food that is easy to grab, that is open to you, invites you closer to it. Storing precut food in Tupperware might make it mushy and unappealing, especially if you are dealing with fruit. If you have to go somewhere, make it easy: bring everything with you—a basket of fruit, cheese, veggies, chips, a linen, your board, and a knife, and cut it up it when you get where you are going. It will be fresh and ready to eat as you are making it. After all, the essence of wood board love is all about the ease and connection too. When you separate yourself from the ease, well, you know what happens. Enjoy, loves x x x x

permission for dinner

So, what *is* for dinner? Does this question bring on an anxious feeling? Whether we know it or not, much of our angst about dinner begins the minute we wake up in the morning. In a nourishing life of becoming, this angst really has no room to thrive. Permission for dinner lives inside a life that feeds you first. For permission to be a regular, everyday part of your life, a practice in living your values is essential. Knowing your values is deeply aligned with knowing who you are and how you want to live. This is everything. Your values support small choices, like what you make for dinner, and the big ones, like what you want to do when you grow up and who you want to love and where you want to live. To know your values is to know yourself and to recognize that you are always changing, evolving, and growing. This is why diets remain diets and fads continue to be fads. To create a life you love takes time, repetition, and a willingness to be the one you've been waiting for. You can go direct toward living your phenomenal life: you can create a culture in your home. There is no need to control, fret, grasp, or make sure of this or that, because your values and boundaries protect you and those around you. You are reflected and held by what you are creating.

Permission for dinner is a nourishing way of living. You are inhaling through the nose and exhaling through the mouth, haaaaaaaaa. There is no rush. This is a forever conversation. There is no destination to get to when you live inside freedom. It just gets better with time and practice. You wake up to where you are. You slow down and listen to your life guiding your every step. You trust life. You let life move you. Living in a nourishing way sets you up to *actually* be nourished. What a concept!

It's like watering one poppy (you) and waking up to a field of gorgeous, thriving poppies (everyone else) all around you. When you are full, you live your life from a full place. You feed the people you love with permission because you are permission! You are no longer sacrificing anything anymore. You are curious about others and how they are living because you have room to listen. There is nothing waiting to be fed inside of you. In this awakening, you move from a life of *regular programming* (mainstream cultureless culture) to nourishing this deeper hunger (with the culture and community you create).

permission and your values

You might be asking yourself, *With all this food out all the time, what if no one eats dinner? What if my kids eat too much? What if I eat too much? What if the food goes bad on the board? What if we keep eating all day long? What if no one eats what I put out? What if . . . ?*

What if has kept me busy for a lifetime. And these are all good questions! Please add any more you have that you don't see here. Get them out onto the page. Once they're all out, let's consider what might be at the root of these *what if* questions. The one question under all of these questions is, drumroll please, WHO AM I? Along with that question is: What are my values? What do I value inside mealtimes with food, health, body, and home? What do I value in the day and in my life? All the stories you have carried, including the ones you have dropped off throughout your journey here, are made of values. They are a mixed bag of historical beliefs, conditions, and strongly held convictions for belonging and surviving. Discerning which values are truly yours and those you have inherited from others is an essential part of becoming you.

Once you get clear on your values, they will support you in making decisions. Values invite you deeper into the *why* of your life, beneath the superficial experiences, to root for something grounded and purposeful. They help integrate *what you are doing* with *how you want to be*. When you inquire about yourself in this deeper way, you can ask the harder questions, making your way to what really matters to YOU. This connects you to revisioning your story—a story that is aligned with how you truly want to live. When you are clear about your values, you get closer to who you are.

Perhaps connection is a value for you and your family. You want to be with your partner, roommate, or kids when everyone gets home. Is food an important part of this for you? Is eating dinner together a value in your home?

If yes, then what are the values around dinner? Do you want to eat in a calm and peaceful environment? Whether or not what you most value is possible for you right now, it is important to be clear about it. You can make decisions from this place of knowing. When you know what you want, regardless of what is happening right now, you can uphold values and intentions that bring you into alignment with your highest vision for your life.

VALUES are basic and fundamental beliefs that guide or motivate attitudes or actions. They help us to determine what is important. Values describe the personal qualities we choose to embody to guide our actions, the sort of person we want to be, the manner in which we treat ourselves and others, and our interaction with the world around us.[24]

Wood board love brings these inquiries and values to the table.

Here are a few different perspectives to consider. You can take what you want and leave the rest. And be gentle here: this is another beginning.

If your kids are hungry before dinner and they are fed with something nourishing, they will be regulated at dinner. This will allow the meal to be more easeful than if they had to wait or are dysregulated, which creates so much stress for everyone. Dinner, most of the time, with the exception of sushi, can be lunch tomorrow. In this freedom, everyone is fed and connection is more accessible.

If you are worried about wasting food, consider that you will still have a body tomorrow, and so many meals are better the next day. Permission is a value-centered way of living. When you know your values, you can flow with everything that is happening. There is no way of connecting, or feeling the love when stress has the microphone!

If you carry pressure about your children eating, you can unpack this in a deeper way inside your own healing. Perhaps this has nothing to do with them, but with your own stories. Whether or not we show how we feel, our kids will pick up on it, so it is important to heal these stories inside of ourselves. Our kids are our greatest teachers. And like I said, we can only do so much in one generation. Breathing *is* something we can do right now. Let's do it together. Your feelings, especially the uncomfortable and anxious ones, will guide you closer to what is here for you. Just you walking toward your doubts and insecurities is a healing. And incredibly brave. I see you. You are not alone. We are in this together.

nourishing you to nourish them

A nourished mama, papa, or caretaker raises a nourished family. Wood board love supports everyone to have their own conversation with food. This is another layer of the intimate terrain we are exploring here. To have your own space to discover your hunger is essential for a healthy relationship with food. When you nourish you, you model exactly that: nourishing yourself. This is the best thing you could ever "say" to your children without using words. Allowing your kids to have their own experience is essential to nourishing their living. They find their way with more ease when the environment is light, loving, and in flow.

Of course, every person and every situation is unique. *Eating* and *nourishing* might be one and the same for you, or they might not. Hunger can come in all shapes and sizes. Often, hunger is not about food—it is about connection, belonging, and feeling loved. If you didn't have this growing up, then you are healing this, too. However, it's important to keep in your heart mind that the language we speak around food can get sticky quickly. We are always changing, and names can lock us into an experience or way of being that doesn't serve anyone. For instance, what is a picky eater? Our culture has become a bit loose-lipped and label-happy with so many terms around food and our kids ("picky," "good," "difficult," "easy" . . .). This kid is this kind of eater and this kid is another kind of eater. What is happening here? Why are we doing this?

Those we consider hard to feed or who don't eat what we cook may want a different connection with us. It may not be about food. Maybe it's the environment or

I
love
us.

what happened at school—there are so many layers to this conversation. What we can do is make room to listen. To slow everything way down, so we can get curious and learn in a new way. You are amazing, and our children are always inviting us to go deeper inside our own lives. Their way of eating, no matter how frustrating and challenging or easygoing it can be, offers you a chance to see them for the complex beings they are. When you make the space to get curious, room is made to heal together. Maybe you are afraid they aren't getting what they need. That is a real story that comes from a real place. The time you carve out here, whatever the outcome, is GOLD. This can be a very complex subject that takes time, tools, and a lot of love, for yourself and your family. I am inviting you to slow down here, to nourish yourself inside all the invitations that call you forward. I love you. I love us.

As we heal, our kids do too. They want to know how to be in their lives. We are showing them the way by learning how *to be* in our lives. Values are not rules. They are ways of being. They come from a heart-centered place. They give you and your family clarity and purpose. When you live from the *outside in*, it uproots you into the old ways of rushing, anxiety, and stress. Values support you to live from the inside out, where what's inside navigates your days and supports your becoming.

hello, body!

to live a value-centered life

To know your values is to integrate who you are with how you live. One way to do this is to carve some time out of your schedule and make a fun ritual of leaning into what YOU value. This is a time to tune in, walk with, sit beside, and move inside what you want for your life and your family. This is something you can do on your own, with your partner, with your entire family, and your business, too!

* Start by tuning in to what you value. You can do this at home, while sitting in a place you love outdoors, or while walking. Think through your entire daily schedule, from the moment you wake up until you go to bed at night. Write it out so you can see what you are actually valuing. When you see the ways you have been spending your time, then you will see what you have been *valuing*. Are these values true to your heart? You can tune in to what is important to you here.

* As you feel ready, put on some music you love and gather your markers and some index cards or pieces of paper you've cut up into smaller pieces.

* Write out all your values (the ones you want to keep), one word per piece of paper, and no more than twenty.

* Once you finish writing, place all of your values on a big table—maybe the dining room table or a coffee table. Walk around the table and take them all in, feeling into all the words you wrote down.

* If you are doing this with others, have everyone write their own individual values, and then they can all be spread out on the table.

* There is no rush here. Take your time, warm a tea, maybe have a piece of cake.

* You can start to move the values around in a hierarchical way, for instance by forming a triangle or a pyramid. Play with where things go and how they feel when they go there. They are all important—you might think one value is more important than another, but once you feel into it, that idea changes!

* Be open to all the possibilities that are here for you and your family.

* It can be helpful to walk away, give yourself space, and then come back to the table. This is such a beautiful way to awaken to your life! Good work!

* Eventually, find your triangle of values: place what you currently value most at the top, with other values forming the sides and base. You can display this somewhere you can see it, using art tape on posterboard or canvas, or even painting your values!

* Remember, your values change and grow as you do. This will support you and your family to live in service to your hearts, your health, and the world!

your heart hunger

Your heart doesn't wait to beat. When you are nourished, the day flows without the stress of your hunger crying like those feral cats at the doorstep of your life. When you feed yourself, your brain regulates itself, which supports your ability to be present and available to your body and the bodies around you. You don't have to wait to feel good. Perhaps some of your old stories are still in the way to feeling unconditional love for yourself. Maybe the thought is, *If I love myself I will not show up for work or pay my bills or take care of my responsibilities. If I love myself, I will set myself free and never do anything again! Who knows?! Maybe never doing anything like that again is the best way to love yourself!*

True love begins with you. When you separate from yourself, you suffer. When you wait to eat, or nourish your body, you suffer. When you disconnect from the journey of being you, you suffer. In this suffering, you will find so many people who are suffering like you, because this way of living is normal in the mainstream culture. No one is questioning suffering. It is in the story of your suffering where your heart hunger might be living. You can't find the ground, feel the soil, or see the beauty around you. You are hoping someone will come, make you a wood board love, and save you. When you look for love somewhere out there, you stay hungry. When you nourish you, everyone is fed.

You are the only one who can feed this heart hunger you carry. Grief lives here, too. I am with you in this grief. This is vulnerable terrain. It is also empowering and enlightening. One of the most powerful things you can do is to simply be with your grief, to see it and hold it in your hands, bathe it and love it for what it is here to teach you. You are the one who can make the wood board love. You are the one who can feed you in the deepest of ways. Your lover, your friends, your children—they can support in the ways they know how, yet this core piece, the place we are inside of here, is all yours. You can model this unconditional landscape of love. When you learn how to nourish your heart hunger, you save your life. When you make a wood board love, beauty water, and get ahead of it with quinoa in the rice cooker, you feed this heart hunger inside of you. This hunger for a caretaker, lovemaker, home-holder. This hunger for a mother. This hunger for YOU! This is your pioneering journey. You are discovering your body as the most phenomenal body. You are changing your mind into a heart mind, a mind guided by the wisdom of your heart. You are becoming you.

heart work
kitchen healer & wood board love how-to tips

♡   **Stain your board.** Stain your board with strawberries, cherries, beets, and all the goodness of your life! You are making memories. Your board is making its way to becoming your legacy. Stain your linens. Stain the pages of this book. Make your mark on what you love. Stains are the stories that we lived and loved, deeply.

♡   **Don't ask me if I am hungry.** Most of the time, you can find me walking into the kitchen and grabbing a wood board off of the wall. I have no idea if I am hungry. What I do know is that I have a body, and it's probably time to feed it. There are other bodies in the house, and at some point we will all have to eat again—so why does hunger get so complicated? So many of us either don't eat, or we wait until someone else is hungry. I have been in homes where you can't see food anywhere. I get hungry when I don't see food out. Where is the food? Why is it hiding? We pay more attention to our stories about food than to our own appetite. Why are we waiting to make food?

When your younger kids are immersed in their play, let them be! When it is time to eat, or even before that, you can make a wood board love and put it out for them. They don't need to know what is happening. This is also for friends, guests, and you, too. When you interrupt the flow to ask if someone is hungry or what they want to eat, this can create stress for both of you, especially with little people! You are not a short-order cook at home, so please stop putting yourself in this role with what you are asking. This can be an edgy idea. Perhaps you've learned to show you care by asking and serving what was asked for. In this way of nourishing, you don't need to ask. Make what you love! When you make a wood board love and offer it freely, the experience of feeding people can feel deeply nourishing. Just put the food out without saying anything—it is like magic! Try it and see. I can't wait to hear what you find.

♡ **I want what you love.** When you make and share what you love, curiosity piques, and nine times out of ten, your kids will want to try it—especially if there is no obligation, pressure, or energy on it. You are creating a culture with wood board love. As you rewrite your story with your values and all you are waking up to here, you allow for everyone to have their own experience. How much they eat or what they choose depends on what you put on the board. This can be healing for everyone. There is freedom and permission here too.

In general, young children are curious and excited about eating. They also don't carry the stories you might about being nourished and fed. When you make what you love and offer it to those you love, everyone feels held in LOVE! Being nourished can happen without anyone *thinking* about it, asking for it, or doing anything other than receiving it. There is nothing to figure out.

It is okay if I don't love everything you put on the board. You can get curious and ask questions. We can have a conversation about food and offerings and expectations—and love! Food and our stories can be emotional, and it's okay if emotions arise. This invites us to get to know each other and lighten the way to more flow, less heaviness. If there are bell peppers on the board or chopped in the crab cake, I will tell you that I don't digest them. I might ask you what you love about them. It is all okay. I love learning about you and what you love. When we release our stories and expectations, we are free to be.

♡ **Get ahead of it.** When we get ahead of our hunger, it can feel like someone else is feeding us. This is already a win. The feeling of *someone else* having your back and your belly can be very healing in the realms of your food story. Getting ahead of your family's hunger is a game changer. It's all about timing with a side of intuition. Feeling that *it is time to have food out* is an important part of this. This is an intuitive muscle that strengthens with practice. Don't wait to be prompted, which could induce stress that can be prevented. This is where wood board love saves the day. It shifts *needs* and *stress* to a rhythm that offers ease and freedom, JOY and FUN! It can feel like a treat, creating a lift in the day. Wood board love can be simple or grand. Either way, when you get ahead of it and don't have to say anything about it, you allow for the medicine to happen. You will see what I mean. I am excited for you!

♡ Let go of the stories that get in the way of connection. You can hear the run-down of how people's kids eat at any school meeting or family dinner. Maybe you too rattle off a tally of each kid, how one kid is a great eater and the other is picky. Like I shared earlier, this can be a deep and intimate terrain. Our words and how we share about our kids, especially in front of them, is vital to how they are seen, felt, and reflected. When it comes to food and how you nourish your life, your view of *how they eat* can be a story they carry in their body forever. You are discovering this here for yourself, too. Your old stories hinder your experience of being connected to you. You are on a journey to get closer to you. In this journey, you are rewriting your stories. This will benefit your children and your lineage. We are in this together.

one more thing: eating together

As parents and caretakers we are *sort of* in charge of the stories that shape our kids. There can be many dynamics present when it comes to eating and food. There is not just one way to heal our food story. But I have found that with the support of ease and beauty, there is space to breathe, be, and connect. These values can create a healing environment. Do you eat with your children? Or if you are caretaking your elderly parents, do you eat with them? Eating together, even if it's a snack, connects us deeply, especially if there is freedom and permission

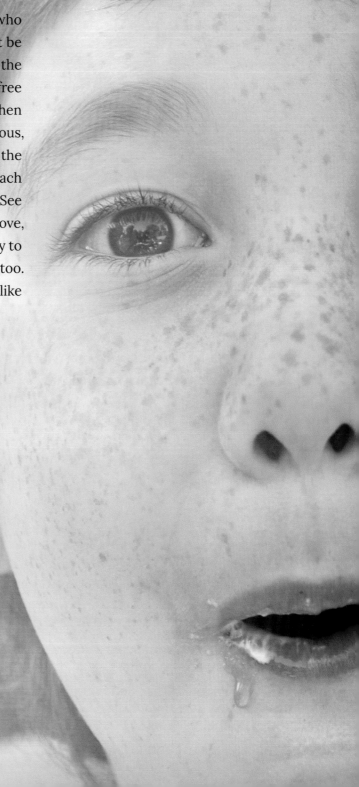

inside the experience. For eaters who have particular needs, there might be stress or expectations that cause the body to freeze up and not feel free to explore their own hunger. When you slow it down and get curious, everyone benefits. Maybe shift the environment—go outside, to the beach or a place that feels less stressful. See what happens. When we feel the love, we might, all of a sudden, feel ready to eat. You are forever changing. Me too. We all go through seasons, just like our Mama Earth.

spoon cake

A cake you can eat with a spoon makes you want to scream-sing permission out the window and into the streets! You are Evita singing about Argentina, yet insert spoon cake for Argentina. *Don't cry for me, oh dear spoon cake. I never left you.* It's okay if you need to go put the song on now; it is so good, just like this cake. This is the kind of freedom I am talking about! Turn on the oven to 350 degrees.

tools

fork or potato masher

a bowl you love

a whisk or the KitchenAid

8- or 9-inch cake pan

parchment paper

rubber spatula

toothpick

a spoon!

gather

1 cup of seasonal fruit (berries, stone fruit, apples and pears, etc.)

⅔ cup (or less) packed light brown sugar, plus some extra for the fruit

½ cup salted butter, melted, plus a bit more for the pan

½ cup whole milk at room temperature

½ tsp salt (unless you are using salted butter)

1 cup King Arthur gluten-free flour

1 tsp baking powder

Mash your fruit with a masher or your hands. Add a bit of sugar to the mix. Let this sit on the side. Gather a bowl you love and mix the melted butter, brown sugar, milk, and salt (if you are using it) with a whisk or the KitchenAid. Then add the flour and baking powder. Keep mixing until smooth. Line your cake pan with parchment paper. Pour the batter into the lined cake pan. Spoon the fruit on top of the batter. Place it in the oven and bake for 20–25 minutes. Do the toothpick test to see if it's fully cooked. When it's ready, remove it from the oven and let it cool in the pan for a bit. Serve warm. Enjoy, loves x x x x

thank you for healing.

first poem (after)

Tell the story of women.
She says

Here is the poem
I haven't written:
I am a secret.

I am the aroma
I am the smell of home
I am on my knees by the fire.

My face is red with a wisdom
that will take lifetimes
to unravel.

Every cell in my cheek
is on fire with love for you.

Asymmetrical now
still in search of balance.

Perform the medicine.
She says

The wind moves
burning my eyes
the smoke of Spirit.

I take it in.
I break open.
I need to wash my hair.

Just keep writing.
She says

I am low on detergent.
Just keep opening.
She says

The magic is
in the breaking open.

The magic is in
the courage to show up
again and again
in the dark
as a secret.

To tell the story
To let the lines of this poem
Teach me everything
I will never know

Done is better than perfect.
She says

This living
it takes a team

As the wood burns,
I let go
I let it all go.

I give fear a warm milky tea.
I put my hand over my chest.
I am checking for a receipt, a pen, a lump.

I explore this new terrain:

skin

scar

flat

full

A mountain range of teachings.

It's not quiet here.

The wood is burning

The chickens chat over lunch

My heartbeat is closer than it's ever been.

And what am I going to make for dinner?

Is this the poem I have yet to write?

For today.

She says

Just for today.

February 2019

"A world lives within you."[25]

John O'Donohue, Anam Cara

part 4

becoming you
a forever
conversation

invitation

You have been on a powerful journey—beginning with the early morning landscape of waking up to your stories, turning on the fire and making your way through the day to feel your body and heal in the kitchen. You are learning how to find yourself inside a culture that needs a nap, a warm cup of love, and a good, long hug. Perhaps our time together has widened your perspective or offered you a basic recipe for remembering who you are, or maybe you are excited to integrate all that you have gathered to make your kitchen and home yours.

You will continue on your path. You will see that your life has a radical kind of intimacy. And when you meet another soul's hunger, you will know how to nourish it as your own. Perhaps you will sit together, make a fire, and share a poem. Maybe you will make a wood board love and ask them what they are ready to let go of. You will remember that we heal in a collective, and there is nothing to fix.

Returning home is the threshold to becoming you. If you are unsure how you will feel at home, remember that you can bring your not knowing with you. This is a part of your healing now.

In this section, you will integrate a practice that is custom-fitted just for YOU. Your journey has led you to this moment right here. Bring all that you have gathered to the soup pot. Stir and steep all that longs to be softened as you return and rebirth an authentic and true life. In chapter 9, "Returning Home," you will have room to rest and recover. As you steep teas and simmer broths, you will discover this gentle, loving way to return again and again to your ever-changing life. As you make your way into chapter 10, you name the closure of this part of your journey as you open the invitation for this forever conversation. It is here that you can bow to your heart, your wisdom, and your healing. Thanking the fire as you blow out the light and close the kitchen for the night.

As you come to the end, you now know, in the deepest parts of you, that you can always begin again. Endings, too, can have old stories lingering around them. You can take it slow and steady here. You can put this book on the kitchen island, on your bedside table, or in the living room—wherever you can see it—so it can remind you of your journey and the practice that continues. You can always open it to what you need to remember. You can leave it open to a recipe you will make in the morning as you close your eyes for the night. Whatever you decide, know that you have shown up for you, which is the deepest loving.

"Well, I think that the threshold—if you go back to the etymology of the word 'threshold,' it comes from 'threshing,' which is to separate the grain from the husk. So the threshold, in a way, is a place where you move into more critical and challenging and worthy fullness. And I think there are huge thresholds in every life.

"I mean I think, for instance, to give a very simple example of it is that if you are in the middle of your life in a busy evening, fifty things to do, and you get a phone call that somebody that you love is suddenly dying—it takes ten seconds to communicate that information, but when you put the phone down, you are already standing in a different world, because suddenly, everything that seemed so important before is all gone, and now you are thinking of this. So the given world that we think is there, and the solid ground we are on, is so tentative.

And I think a threshold is a line which separates two territories of spirit, and I think that very often how we cross is the key thing."[26]

John O'Donohue

chapter 9

returning home

Haaaaaaaaa. Returning home from a powerful journey can hold many feelings. You might want to dive back in fast or stop everything and stare at the wall for a month. You are naming how you feel as you put your bags down and show up at the front door. You are listening to you. You are full of poems, ways of being, and recipes for cakes to rise and bake. Usually in a transition home, you might like to hit the ground running. The cultural or familial expectation is to *get it together and go back to work*. Yet the ground you are coming home to is breaking wide open. You have journeyed through a new way of living as a healing. Maybe you want to get your hands in the soil, aerate what has been packed down for so long. You are placing your hand on your heart as you stand in your foyer looking for yourself. You ask your partner, friend, lover to draw you a bath with herbs—eucalyptus and rose and a scoop of Epsom salt. You want to breathe in the love you have found as you slowly walk down the hallway to the bathroom.

You already took so much time off, and now you want to take *more* time to transition? I mean . . . *who are you?* Exactly. Greatest question ever. Keep asking it! Especially now, you are reshaping the mold you walked into this book with. You are softening and rooting to and for yourself in the best way. You might become someone who needs more time. PS: every single person in the world needs more time. You are more YOU than you have ever been. Go gently as you notice what emerges for you. Will you allow yourself to continue to become who you are? Keep yourself close.

heart work
a letter to your remembering

One way to keep yourself close is to remember your journey, which is also to value your experience. This is another deep loving for yourself. Writing a letter to your heart is a beautiful way to re-member, value, and in turn make an offering to your healing and living.

♡ Gather your special stationary or paper you love, an envelope, and a stamp.

♡ Find a comfortable place where you can write a letter. Begin with lighting your candle.

♡ Write your address on the envelope and place the stamp.

♡ Start the letter with *Dear* (your name).

♡ Something like this:
  Dear jules,
  I am back home and I have been thinking about you.
  I never want to forget . . .

♡ Really let go here—share every single thing that wants to come forward. It might be what you learned on your journey, in this book, or any powerful experiences you want to share from this time. Or any time of transition you are inside of.

♡ Make this a ritual and take your time.

♡ Head to the post office, or put it in a mailbox when you run your next errand across town or go on a trip!

♡ You will receive this letter in the perfect time. Your letter will go on a journey to make its way back to you.

♡ You can open it and put it on your altar. Reread it whenever you need to get close to you.

"To believe your own thought, to believe that what is true for you in your own private heart is true for all human beings—that is genius."[27]

Ralph Waldo Emerson

rest & repeat

You know how they talk about *Savasana* being the most difficult pose in yoga? It is also the most powerful. *Savasana* is the final, resting pose in most yoga practices; it is also considered the most important pose. The literal translation for *Savasana* is "Corpse Pose." You might not feel like today is the day you want to practice dying; yet, as you become you, there are parts of you dying. In returning home, you will see how you have been changed. This can feel like a death. It can also feel pretty vulnerable in a culture that doesn't know how to breathe or, in other words, slow down and live. To "consciously die" or rest intentionally for about fifteen to twenty minutes is a way to pause and support all of you inside this transitional time. To let the mind truly settle, to give your nervous system a bath of your breath, is deeply restorative for your living. My yoga teachers, Shosha and Io, make so much time for this in their classes. Gathering the blanket, the eye pillow, the bolster, they say, "Take your time to get it just right for you today, and make sure you are warm." There have been many days when you could find me resting on the kitchen floor, a kind of "kitchen Savasana" as I wait for the kettle to boil or the veggies to roast. I am always in there, so why not lie down and take a few minutes to breathe and settle?

To take a nap in our culture is a revolutionary kind of activism. Perhaps you are in the flow of your naps and you can sleep anywhere. Or you went to medical school, or any intensive training, where you learned to sleep standing up with a coffee in your hand. In any case, you probably need a rest. Me too. Rest is a vital ingredient in returning home to your body and your life. How do you integrate rest into your day-to-day life?

The ways you rest sustain how you live. You can lie down to face the sun, feeling your body melt into the warmth of the ground. You can go outside and feel your feet in the grass, visualizing roots grounding you as they make their way to a well of water in the dark, rich soil. You can make a fire, sit and watch it burn. Feel its powerful medicine and let it move you to rest your gaze. You can look out your favorite window and watch the hummingbirds find the sweet nectar in the feeder hanging off the orange tree. And like I shared, a restful moment can also happen in the kitchen. There are many ways to go slower and find a rhythm that can hold you gently in rest. One of these ways is in steeping teas. There is no rush in steeping. They are synergistic—steeping and resting can happen together. Most of us carry the fantasy of having more rest-filled days. We long for our days to slow down inside all that we are doing and being. Even in this moment right here, as you are reading and taking this in, feel your body. Listen for your breath. Your awareness brings you here, and this is where rest can be. Look at us resting here together.

steeping tea

There is so much magic in steeping. It is a transformation of the most basic and simplest ingredients. You can go slowly here. Steeping tea is a transfer of energy and love from plants that have grown through the dark into the light, blossoming in the sun, to your body. It is everything you are as you make your way home on this journey. You are feeling you—physically, mentally, soulfully, spiritually. You are bringing your essence to your bigger body like the herbs to this big Ball jar of hot water. You are creating tinctures to sip and take in as you recover and discover you again.

tools

kettle or pot

big Ball jars that can withstand
   boiling water

linen towel, trivet, or cover of some kind

wood spoon

gather

all the herbs, dry and fresh, that you love

sage honey or a honey you love

here are some ideas: mint, lemon verbena
   and mint, thyme, thyme and mint,
   hibiscus and elderberry, chamomile

Fill the kettle with water and set it to boil. Cut herbs from the garden or gather them from the market, and rinse them off.

Put out everything you'll need on the counter or island. Make sure your glass vessels are made to handle hot water! Jars intended for canning, like Ball jars, are tempered so they can withstand high heat without cracking. When the water is ready, pour it into the jars with herbs and let it sit with a cozy or trivet over the vessel. In a few minutes, add a wood spoon scoop of honey if you wish. Stir that in, and let it steep some more. Do not put ice in with very hot water as the glass might crack. Wait till it cools down a bit. Easy does it. Take your time. Slow it down. Let yourself steep here, too. Enjoy, loves x x x x

You are creating a rest practice. For many of us, this is easier said than done. I saw firsthand how challenging it can be for women to rest during our retreats. There was a "TIME TO REST" scheduled on the syllabus in big, bold letters. Women who had traveled from all over the country to the retreat were finally away from their busy lives, their families' needs, and all the noise, chaos, and stress that went into them getting to the retreat. All they wanted to do was rest. Yet, in the space allotted for rest, I would see them connecting with each other outside, making another tea, walking together and laughing. I walked around, like a loving "rest sergeant," reminding them to take a break, kindly suggesting they go back to their rooms and restore themselves before the next session. I would make several rounds, practically herding them (softly) to their rooms. I realized after a few retreats that it wasn't happening. Resting is intimate work. To leave your relationship with doing and move into alone time with your breath is a big leap, especially if you find yourself in a gorgeous place with incredible

people you are falling in love with. And maybe this is also rest. Rest is a muscle that regulates the nervous system. Connecting and laughing are also ways to tend this. Finding *your way* of resting is important for a smooth and loving transition home.

self-care is "we-care"

In discovering *your* way of resting, just being in the inquiry of what feels restful is a deep caring for yourself. Like everything else we've been moving through, this might entail revisioning an old story. How you care for yourself is custom, and it takes courage in a culture like ours. My friend Elizabeth shares about this idea of making *breathing room* inside our lives. She says that meditating or getting a massage is one thing, but to consistently give yourself breathing room inside your day is to change your life. This is what your journey to becoming you is all about. Creating your life with breathing room integrated everywhere helps you cross the threshold to your whole self. You no longer need to separate, shut down, or, even worse, make yourself sick to get the rest you need. Your practice of resting serves the world. You may know it as self-care, yet it is really "we-care"—care for the whole of yourself is care for the whole of the world.

hello, body!

limiting beliefs & borrrring stories . . .

I will offer a few of the limiting beliefs I've encountered to get you going, and you can add yours to the list.

* Caring for myself is for later on, when I have time. It is also not necessary *all the time*. Too much taking care of me is selfish. There is a limit to caring for me, as I have things to do.

* Buying or gathering flowers is a luxury, a privilege, for people who have time, money, or a party to throw. Who has time to even talk about this?

* Spending time with the earth is for people who have time, or for a vacation I can only take if I keep working.

* Seeking and receiving support is for people who have money. And for an emergency.

Which ones resonate with you? If these inspired more, write them here.

Whatever your *chosen limiting belief* might be, it is in the way to your becoming. And whatever seems to be blocking your path to healing is usually *the* path to your healing, so it's a win-win when you show up for yourself.

Okay, let's slow this down. The limiting thought or belief that comes up the most is the one to follow first. It is the caution tape wrapped around the life you long for. As you continue to unpack lineages of borrrring stories, you create more space to care for yourself and your family. Watch out, as these thoughts hide out in your most profound ideas. *What you know* is usually a million miles away from what you actually *do for yourself*. The wisdom ways of being and caring were held inside circles of elders. There were no other options. Their self-care was their care for Mother Earth. They only knew the "we" mindset. Since they modeled this kind of care to the younger generations, it led to the whole tribe thriving. We have strayed quite far from this. Our grief and longing for those deeply integrated ways lives in our bodies; they are still a part of our intuitive knowing. I believe much of our grief is in not knowing how to meet that deeper calling inside the shape and rhythm of our days today. What has been conditioned wins over what we deeply hunger for. And here we are, in therapy about our mothers, our schedules, and our lives. We can feel lost because we are lost. We are looking for the reflection for how to breathe and come back to ourselves inside the day. We are hungry for the love, consistency, and freedom that wasn't available when we were growing up. You may have found yourself completely separate from the Earth's wellness as well as from your own. Living separately from Her has caused you, and us, so much stress, illness, and disease. The Earth is me and you and us. Self-care is we-care. We-care is a direct line to caring for Mother Earth. When we make our way to a "we" way of being and living, we can get out of the mind and closer to the body. In doing this, we live from the heart mind. When we get closer to the earth and what really matters, we are healing the whole. When you heal, I heal. When I heal, you heal. When we all heal, the world heals.

returning to the kitchen

Speaking of being in therapy about our mothers—hello, kitchen! In returning home, resting, steeping, and caring for yourself, you might find yourself in the heart, the hearth, the warm love that is your kitchen. You know how to do it: find your feet, light the candle, and invite the fire to begin again. In this returning,

you are *turning again and again* toward yourself. Remember the whirling dervishes? You continue to rewrite this story as you feel into the rhythm you want to return to. What feels like home? How do you want to honor your returning? How do you want to turn on the fire?

As you transition, you can take a day, or a week, or a whole lifetime to create the support you need. Take the time you need. Move whatever thoughts are in the way of getting closer to you. Support your emotional *and* physical immune systems. What is the way for you to transition home and feel the ground supporting you? Open the freezer and find those chicken bones you froze from the last roasted chicken. Open the fridge and take out all your veggies. Ask the neighbor for what they have in spades that they can offer you for your soup. Perhaps this is a *stone soup* moment. Ask the land, the neighbors, and a friend to bring you a few ingredients to help you ground in to being home. Find the slow cooker and plug it in.

bone broth (or any broth) in the slow cooker

This is the easiest thing to make, especially in a slow cooker. Put all the ingredients into the base or pot and add a few cups of water. Turn it to slow cook on high for sixteen hours. The longer it cooks, the better it will be. It will move to the warm setting as the time begins to run out. If you can put it on again for another sixteen hours, even better. Over time you will see a deep golden color emerge. This is what you are moving toward. You are moving toward the gold inside of you.

tools
slow cooker or a big cast-iron pot
pot holders
ladle
teacup
linen towel

gather

bones of 1 chicken and/or other animal bones (you can mix them)

a few unpeeled carrots

1 whole onion with peel

1 Tbsp apple cider vinegar

any veggie scraps or peels

some ginger or garlic or both

2 bay leaves

Put it all together and press START! I love having a teacup of this in the midday or later in the afternoon. It takes the place of another milky love tea. Every sip is grounding for me and my body. This is the medicine for returning, for resting, for restoring. This is also vital medicine for after a birth or any surgery.

As the aroma of the broth permeates the house, you begin to feel held, again. As you know by now, this is everything. You remember yourself and move forward from this grounded place. Feeling held as you make your way through another transition is where you begin to meet trust—even if just for a moment. Trust quietly grows as you steep the tea, cook the soup, and extract everything you can from the bones of your stories. You are learning how to feel this trust and grow that golden hue of faith around you as you keep awakening into the love that you are.

"My work is loving the world."[28]

Mary Oliver

a forever conversation

Wow,
 wow,
wow,
 mazel tov, love!
You made it!
 I made it!
 We made it.

Oh dear amazing reader, you have shown up here, inside every page, with your intentions, your love for you, and your hunger to feed those you love. Perhaps you have found yourself in the unknown a lot more than you expected to. Maybe you had no idea that showing up is how you get here, there, everywhere. Showing up is how you change your mind. Showing up is the way to become you. Good news: you no longer need to take some big trip or fantasy journey to find yourself. You are with you all the time. The dread has diminished and the anxiety is finding a new language for living, and you are in the flow of a life that is for you. Freedom arises in the knowledge that no matter what comes down the path, it is an invitation for you to get closer to your life. This is a healing. This is a forever conversation.

gathering a healing team

Healing is a living you create. Living is a healing you cook up and serve to your-self and those you love. It is not something you do *over there*. It is right here, in every moment you wake up to, in every schedule you fill, in every meal you cook, in every decision you make. It is a vow you take to be in conversation with yourself at all times. And by *conversation* I mean full sensory engagement: speaking with, feeling, see-ing, and hearing. In our culture, relating to ourselves in this way is not necessarily trending yet, which makes it difficult to access for those who would never consider it as an option. Or even worse, who judge it from afar.

To heal is to become sound, healthy again, or put right; to alleviate, correct.[29]

To be held and reflected and supported in your life is essential to your growth. For this journey, and forever, it's so important to have a team! And once you say yes to a team, which might take a minute or longer, be prepared for the surprise interventions from strangers and those you love, too. The universe and all that surrounds you is ON YOUR SIDE. This is just physics and gravity and the stuff of galaxies rooting for your life. When we say YES to gathering support for our best lives, all the energy says YES, too. Remember how your healing is the world's healing? This is not some wacky idea. If you sit with it, it makes all the sense in the world. I am sure you have already experi-enced this throughout your journey—and it doesn't stop here. This is just the beginning (again). Your YES and all that will support you is limitless—it never runs out. You can't fail. All you have to do is show up for you. The energy will meet you wherever you want to go. Your thoughts might be really stuck in place, so we might need a little salve, like some olive oil (cake), to set you free.

In gathering your team, you will meet people who have been where you are, who have a headlamp that shines on an area in your life you need to look at. You might meet a wisdom witch disguised as a cashier at Trader Joe's, or fairies in street clothes who can show you the way to your deepest self. All you have to do is show up. You don't have to believe in anything other than yourself. You can just say yes every day to the change that is already happening. Being specific, intentional, and grounded are vital here. You are not just going with the flow and seeing where it takes you. You are the flow, grounded in your YES with purpose in your heart and service on your mind.

There are many ways to heal, and for that very reason, you need others who can contribute their particular wisdom. Your body, mind, emotional terrain, and nervous system are all places of healing, just to name a few. You now know that you carry stories from lineages and legacies that go wayyyyy back. You have a home, a job, relationships, a community, and our Mother Earth to love and care for. There is no job out there that would consider just one person for all of this. You need a team!

When you say *I am fine* yet go on living as though everything is urgent while not stopping to breathe or fuel yourself, you suffer. Our collective illness comes from our deep, individual hunger. Why is healing or gathering a team only for emergencies, or for other people? Perhaps we need to redefine the "emergency" story so many of us have

on a loop in our minds. Let's reweave that loop with intention, love, and we-care. Maybe part of your story is that you don't want to cause a fuss or draw attention to yourself, or that you don't deserve this kind of care. If healing was a part of mainstream living, taking good care of ourselves wouldn't seem like a big deal. We are getting there, one love tea at a time.

When you value work and money and a feeling of urgency over the body, being, and rest, you suffer. It doesn't have to be so extreme. Every single part of you is essential to the whole. When one part of you is not well, all of you suffers. When you are not well, I suffer. When I am not well, you suffer. When you create a team to hold you, reflect you, support you—you heal. It isn't necessarily about "needing" it or not; it's about supporting your basic needs. This is also a pioneering heart mind place . . . until it's not. Athletes and high-powered business people have teams, so why not you? The story of doing it yourself is more borrrring and painful than any other story out there. Gathering a team nourishes that shape and guides you to an entirely new perspective. The only thing this requires is your deepest YES for yourself, especially when you don't see how it can happen. Moving toward your truest YES creates the most incredible room and ability for you to heal, grow, and thrive. Your YES and the envisioning that comes with it is real, and it will change your life if you want it to.

We all need a team.

We all need support in a world that is falling apart at the seams.

Bring it on.

What does your team look like? You can start with what you need and want most in the moment. Therapy? Acupuncture? Bodywork? Life coach? Kitchen healer? There are incredible practitioners that might offer a few things in one person. A team is a group of people who can hold space for you and your becoming. They consist of trusted guides, healers, elders, doctors, and flashlight holders bringing the light to what you can't see on your own. A team is a group of people you trust with your life moving forward. You might have an amazing family and dear friends—they are not the team you are gathering here. They already have a name: they are your friends and family.

Your team is made up of people who can do the deep work with you without getting emotionally involved the way family and friends tend to. They hold you accountable and will witness your transformation. If you are *waiting for an emergency* to gather your team, here it is: living your life, the one that is right here as you wake up to yourself, is the emergency. You don't need to wait any longer. The time frame of your precious and powerful life is unknown. Now is the new later. Go for it. Go for YOU, your family, your lineage and the world. There are so many ways to call in a team depending on the clarity, desire, passion, time, and bandwidth you have available. A team consists of two or more people—YOU and one phenomenal person—to begin. Start by saying YES to yourself and calling in what you need. Be specific. Don't leave it up to *whatever* because *whatever* is what you will get. Clarity is everything. Watch out! Here it comes!

heart work
gathering a team

Healing is a reciprocal relationship. You can't fail when you say yes to your healing. All you have to do is show up and say yes to yourself. Say yes to the places you feel called to go, teams you want to seek out, other people who are on the path. Get curious about what actually feels good to you. This process of finding your team might not go as quickly as you want it to. Stay the course. Showing up daily is the way to get to where you want to be. A team consists of more than one person. Start with finding one and go from there.

♡ Find a place where you love to write, that is quiet and supports your centering.

♡ Light a candle and offer your listening to the fire.

♡ Settle into your body and sit with your eyes closed for a few minutes, breathing in and out. Take all the time you need here.

♡ Begin to tune in to what you want in your first teammate and/or in your whole team. You might already know exactly who you have been wanting to work with, but what they are offering isn't aligned with your schedule or your bank statement, and you have no idea how to make it happen. You are not alone! Reach out to them anyway, write them from your heart, use your voice! Seek out what is possible for YOU. This is such intimate terrain. Be gentle with yourself as you share what you love about their work and how it has changed your life. Ask them how you can work with them. You will learn so much in this action, let alone in the magic that will come! You have nothing to lose. You are so worth your time in discovering what is possible here. This is a powerful healing in itself.

♡ If you are not sure who your first teammate is, write down everything you want in a team. Be specific. Your heart wisdom knows the way.

♡ Place this paper on your altar so you can look at it when you sit or pass by.

♡ This is just the beginning; you are always changing.

♡ Feel this deep love and gratitude for showing up for yourself!

valuing you

Choosing to heal, grow, and thrive in our lives is brave work. You are not broken. You are alive and incredible. You are seeking to fully inhabit your life and change your mind. You are feeling your heart in everything you do. Your culture can't reflect or hold you in this because it is as hungry as you are, if not more. There are so many shiny things to distract you from your truth, yet every day you are making time to care for yourself. It is no longer an event. It is becoming a practice. You are valuing you. I mean . . . you are gathering a team now!

In a life of valuing yourself, you get to know all the voices on repeat in your head—even the ones that are so entrenched in the leftover residue of the old story, you might still mistake them for your own inner voice. These are usually the heaviest hitters. Their opinions about how you look in the mirror claim a seat at the table right next to the Buddha inside of you. Your extra loving triceps and that deep meditation practice deserve equal tending and respect. What are they saying to each other? No more separating ourselves, not even with the little voices that live deeply woven inside of us. This is your chance to let it all gooooo! Let it truly go. There is no voice that's too small. I am inviting you to nourish the divide inside of you. What other parts of you are inside this forever conversation? Write them down here.

hello, body!

nourishing the divide inside

* Warm tea.

* Light fire.

* Find your feet.

* One haaaaaaaa breath at a time.

* Being with what is here.

* Being with your breath.

* Being with your body.

* Being with your resistance.

* Being with Spirit, the Earth, the fearless faith you are growing and tending here.

* Being with the gerbil wheel inside of you, the traveling circus of stories that spin like gold to invite you to get closer to becoming you.

* In being with all of you, you can begin again and again.

And here you are, coming into the kitchen to warm up some milk and cinnamon and call it a night. As we begin to close our circle here, I am remembering those long evening conversations with a dear friend or an intimate group of women on retreat, enjoying a warm something around the kitchen island as the day was coming to a close. When we share about what is vital in our lives and the stories that got us here, we become a healing balm for each other. I love thinking about us, you and me, in the kitchen, having this forever conversation. As we show up to heal ourselves, we heal each other. Repeating this and so many other swatches of this language fabric you have gathered makes room for the old stuff to move out and the newer you to rebirth and reshape into the unconditional love that you truly are. The light is dim and the candles are lit. I am pouring milk into the little copper pot as you gather your vessel from the cabinet, for something warm in the palm of your hand. Just like how we started.

cinnamon milky

tools

a small pot

whisk

teacup or vessel
  of some kind

gather

any kind of milk

cinnamon

This is one of Beauty's favorite things to have before bed. It also sates a sweet little hunger that likes to show up for many of us close to bedtime. Put the stove on low—any kind of milk can heat up and burn very quickly. Gather a small pot you love; if you don't have one, perhaps this is one of those must-have moments. You can search for "milk warming pot" or "butter warmer." Get ready for cuteness galore. The little pots with the pouring lip are the sweetest. Maybe it can be a journey gift for you and your showing up for yourself here. Warm your milk for just a few minutes. If you see the top forming a film, it is time to mix and pour. Add your cinnamon on top. I like to whisk this in the teacup or mug until there's froth on top. You can also use a milk frother here too. It is the simple things that heal in the deepest of ways. Enjoy, loves x x x x

becoming you

To become is *to begin to be*. Yes, please. I love beginning to be. I love that we are always on a path of beginning, even when we are inside an ending. The timing may not be exactly how you thought it would or how you saw it going; yet a life happening *for you* is the life that is right here, moving you toward your becoming. And it is always right on time. No matter what you do, *being* invites you closer to your heart space, and so does beginning. As you create a practice to lean in and listen to your longing, you will learn that you are forever in the unknown as you heal and live and breathe and grow. And life will continue to invite you forward.

When you open to the Earth around you, with Her beauty and immense offerings, you can find your way back to yourself. Every time you feel this, you will experience yourself in a deeper way. When how you see your life changes, your mindset changes. When your mindset changes, your life transforms. As you turn on the fire, feel your feet on the floor, and heal in the ways that nourish you, you offer yourself to the Earth. In truth, we are all working for Her. She is our bigger body and the unconditional mother we have deeply longed for. There is nothing more to know.

Your awakening is your becoming. Your becoming is an offering to the Earth. This is not only how you live your life; it is also why you become who you are. When you become you, you shed and unravel all that heaviness, and over time, you are lighter to carry. You are not broken. You were never broken. You are whole, and holy, love. And in this wholeness, and holiness, you are no longer afraid to love you. As my healer, Dr. Eileen Kenny, says, "Life loves you. Life has you. Life is on your side." I can't seem to hear this enough. Every single time she says it, something inside of me shifts, in alignment to heal again. I hope this happens for you here, in seeing and feeling the visual language through art and poetry, and showing up intentionally for your heart work. May this continue to shift you into your deepest living.

As you gather your things, picking up your basket and taking your last sip of love tea for now, may you feel the truth of all truths: you are enough. You are beyond enough. You are the most magnificent being. Your life's journey is powerful and profound and precious. This is now your healing field. I see you and all that you are growing. There is nothing like tending your own deep belonging. I feel this here with you. I hope you feel it, too. The medicine of slowing down and saying yes to your life is the way to nourishing your wisdom. It really is a forever conversation. You are a sacred offering. You are a radical kind of intimacy. You are becoming you.

flourless chocolate cake

May you always celebrate this life and your forever becoming. This is one of those cakes that works every time. What I mean is, you can't mess this up. It's delicious no matter what you think is happening, just like your healing. And you want to gather the very best ingredients just like all the amazing people you are going to gather for your team. Start with the oven at 350 degrees.

tools

double boiler (or a
   saucepan filled with
   an inch or two of
   water and a Pyrex
   bowl inside over top)
rubber spatula
8-inch cake pan lined
   with parchment paper

KitchenAid or
   hand mixer
2 large bowls
toothpick
cooling rack
cake plate or any
   plate you love

gather

10 oz organic and
   amazing dark
   chocolate
10 Tbsp unsalted or
   salted butter

1 cup cane sugar
7 large organic eggs
1 tsp pure vanilla extract
1 tsp salt

First, melt the chocolate. You can use a double boiler, or make a DIY double boiler by bringing an inch or two of water to a simmer over medium-low heat, then placing a glass Pyrex bowl over top so that it fits snugly and doesn't touch the water. Mix the chocolate with your spatula as it melts. Once it's melted, set it to the side.

Butter the pan and line it with parchment paper. Put it to the side too. Then, using the KitchenAid or a hand mixer and a bowl, beat the butter and the sugar into a creamy whipped situation. Get this light and loving! Then add one egg YOLK at a time, putting the whites into a large bowl beside you. Scrape the batter down the sides of the bowl as needed with your spatula. Add vanilla. Mix it briefly and let it be for a minute.

If you are using a hand mixer, clean it and gather it again for this mixture of egg whites. Or you could do this by hand (or really it should be called *by arm*). Add a bit of salt to the egg whites and mix until you start seeing stiff peaks. This is a great time to release any feelings if you want to offer them over to the egg whites.

Now we move into the folding realm. The first time I did this, I was impatient and so incredibly annoyed. After many times of learning how to fold, I realized it was an invitation to slow it way down. HAAAAAAAAA. Thank you, folding. Here is this powerful time for you to slowwww down. Pour a little bit of the egg whites into the batter, folding them by hand, little by little with your rubber spatula. Take some haaaaaaaaa breaths and allow for these two mixes to slowly get to know each other. This is your practice of becoming. A little at a time. It feels so good when you surrender to it and let it move you. At some point, it will all be integrated into one bowl of silky batter, and you will pour it into your pan. Now place it in the oven. You have about 30–40 minutes to bake this lovefest. Make sure the top is firm when you move it a bit; it shouldn't shake like Jell-O. Give it a minute and then take a knife to move around the edges of the pan. Put the cake on the cooling rack to cool. This is an epic cake that will take you to the next level. I will meet you there. Enjoy, loves x x x x

radical intimacy

It can be so loud inside
this life ready in every moment.

All I want to do is bare my skin
put my feet in Your soil
melt like salted love butter in Your palm
stir with You inside a worn wooden spoon.

The weathered wisdom of being
lets all the grips that came before me,
go.

As my wet face nourishes this porous place,
the highest cheek bones of this holy terrain
a landscape we like to call our own.

Ahhhh the view from here!

Colonizing our deepest longing at
a longitude of not knowing anything
a latitude of today's to-do list.

There is poety everywhere.

Vats of fear lead me astray.
wet tea bags hang from my backpack
to steep in the sun
an immersion for everone.

There is no degree for a woman like me
I am a radical kind of intimacy.

As I carry this calling,
I listen for the way:

You
Me
Her

A spirit of willingness,
Slowing it down where it hurts
Gathering the most basic ingredients

I strip what I can.

My body
Your body
Her body

There is nothing to do here.
There is nothing to fix.

I am a forever conversation.

Beginning again, and again,
I am the inquiry.
I am divine urgency.

I am becoming.
A radical kind of intimacy.

December 2019

GRATITUDE

Oh dearest book, thank you for choosing me to birth you into the world. And guess what crossing a threshold, and allll the liminal spaces in between, takes? A team! I love a team! And I love my team! I want to shout it from the rooftops and the peaks of every ocean wave. The only way this book is here, in this way, in your hands, is due to having a team in many realms. First to my body! Thank you, body! And to the team that has held, supported, and loved my body through this fierce and tender journey. Thank you forever to Dr. Eileen Kenny and the Alta Dena Healing Arts tribe of amazing humans and healers, Dr. Marsha Connor, Dr. Jeannie Shen, Vicky, Shay, Darcy, Gary, Shosha and Io.

To all the elders and healers at Daré, Revisioning Medicine, and everyone in our powerful counsel of the 19 Ways. To Deena Metzger for offering me the language for the impossible, and showing me how to listen for the story in the unknown. To Sharon Simone for modeling the fiercest ways to find the light inside the darkest parts of the journey. Thank you for continuing to show me how to feel for what is being offered.

To all the word fairies, proposal doulas, and book midwives! Haaaaaaaaa! Thank you, Elise Loehnen, for coming over to walk in the backyard, find your breath, and let me inspire your fire in the kitchen. Thank you for writing about this powerful work and planting a few more seeds that helped grow this moment right here. Thank you, Cassie Jones, for reaching out to ask if I wanted to write a book, and for introducing me to Alison Fargis and the Stonesong team! Thank YOU Alison for saying YES inside the unknown with me. We did it! Thank you for every conversation as I walked "around and around the pool" of writing this book, not knowing how to dive in. Thank you to Joelle Hahn, Jacqueline Suskin, Amely Greeven, and Moon Love for all the time and support as I walked around the pool a few more times. Until I finally dove in! Thank you to Sophy Dale for your loving encouragement and doula support. To Haven Iverson for your YES! And your patience and guidance in showing me the way through this book, the process and what it needed to say. Thank you Rachael Murray for your open heart smiling as I opened my front door to you and our incredible and intimate photo shoot team. Thank you to the entire Sounds True Team—those I met via zoom, in person, inside the book, and whom I will continue to meet! I bow to you and all that you held and supported inside these pages. To the incredible women behind the lens: Molly Donna Ware, I am tearing up just thinking of you. Thank you for healing. Your healing made it possible for you to capture all that is here. Thank you for coming over to find the light, again and again. Miranda, your hunger, your love, your willingness is inside so much of this book. Thank you for saying YES. Joe, thank YOU for walking through the fire! Lisa, thank you for being with me in so many beginnings. I cherish you. To the writing teachers that have held my non-linear way with words for many years, thank you for supporting me to keep writing no matter what: Bruce Gelfand, Ann Randolph, Wendy Hammers.

Thank you to all the women who have come to this work, nourished in my kitchen, sat by the fire, healed on retreat, or transformed inside personal and powerful journeys. I bow to your brave and profound healing. I am the luckiest to be witness to YOUR YES. You continue to teach me what this work is about and how we heal in a collective. Thank you, Patreon Community, for walking by my side, supporting me through this writing journey. Thank you, Gather You, for your wholehearted healing. You continue to show up and reshape your lives with me every Tuesday.

To my heart holders, my friends, phenomenal supportive beings who see, hear, feel, and love me inside the messy beauty of this life: thank you for healing alongside me. I love you! To my family of origin and all the invitations offered to me and us to heal our lineage: thank you for healing, and I love you!

To Rachel Langer, your healing and how you held me made it possible for me to see my way. I am forever grateful for you and our work together. I love you! Kimmers, your open heart, your unconditional listening, and our laughter are soft places for me to land. Thank you for our friendship. It is one of my greatest gifts. Thank you for healing with me. I love you! Moon, your intuitive, open, and loving hands holding me inside this process helped me navigate the early days of structure and fonts and colors with a few tears and so much healing laughter. Thank you for seeing this book before I could. I loved writing together (sometimes across the country) in tandem, learning from each other every step of the way. Thank you for healing with me. I love you!

Mama, thank you for giving me life. Dad, you are with me every day. Ocean Love and Beauty Cleopatra, thank you for teaching me everything I still don't know. You are my whole heart. You are everything I ever wanted and more. I love you! Hunners, thank you for going on your journey to heal and become you.

Thank you to the Tongva land in South Pasadena and Ojai, all the wood burning fires, all the beings, hummingbirds, chickens, Hossy, Sammy Bear, all the freedom parrots, hawks, the one owl in the night that held me when I couldn't sleep, and the most exquisite moth who has shown up right here at the front door inside these last few pages. Thank you, Spirit, for continuing to show me the way. Thank you, Sunny, for holding me and our family.

Thank YOU for being here, healing with me and becoming who you truly are. I love YOU and I love US.

Here are a few more tools of the kitchen healer trade. Setting up your kitchen to be a place that reflects who you are is about surrounding yourself with what you love and feel connected to in the best way. Aligning what is on the outside with who you are becoming on the inside connects you with your values. You know the way: light your candle, feel your feet, and find your body as you create a space that will heal you.

Kitchen Tools & Values

Lean in and get closer to what you love.

Check in with your heart when making a choice.

Consume consciously: be Earth-centered as you choose your tools for the kitchen. Ask: does this help or hurt our Mother Earth?

Choose the tools that best support you. You don't need a lot.

Choose the best quality because YOU are the best quality!

Gather what you love.

Wood

♡ Wide wood bowls that feel like a soft place to land

♡ Wood spoons that feel good in the palm of your hand; have a variety of sizes for stirring, serving, and sautéing

♡ Wood boards you love: a few on hand or hanging on the wall for wood board love, an onion/garlic/meat board, small ones for a spoon rest, boards for fruit altars on the dining table or as an elevated altar for the olive oil, open salt, and butter near the stovetop

Glass

♡ Ball jars in every size for drinking, storing, gifting, steeping, as a vase, etc.

♡ French terrines for grains, pastas, snacks, teas, coffee, sugar, flour, granola, crackers, and grab-and-go for school and travel

♡ Glass Tupperware for fridge and freezer (let go of all the plastic—it's time)

Steel

♡ Wide & round sauté pans so you can stir and sauté with freedom
♡ Wide pots (sauce & sauté) with two handles for sautéing, scrambling eggs, and cooking oatmeal, rice, soups, and stews
♡ Small pots, copper, enamel, and/or steel, for warming milk and tea or melting butter
♡ Cast-iron pans to have on the stovetop and in the oven for roasting and baking
♡ Small spatula that fits in your hand, perfect for pancakes, eggs, latkes
♡ Small whisk for frothing warm milk, baking, or mixing something light
♡ Baking sheets of different sizes: one or two small, one or two medium, and one large
♡ Cake pan—you can gather an 8" and a 9" (I have two of each), if you want to attempt a layered cake (I have yet to, but I love that it's possible when I am ready)

Clay

♡ Pinch pots for salt, tops, seeds, pits, and everything
♡ Wide bowls so you can see your food in the fridge and to place on food altars
♡ Bowls and plates of every size that you love to look at and eat on
♡ Teapots in colors you love
♡ Egg holders for vitamins and olive pits
♡ Vessels, cups, and mugs for tea you love love love
♡ Casserole dishes you love for roasting, baking, and serving
♡ Pie plates for quiche, pie, roasting, and baking
♡ Cake plates for berries, fruit, altars, kitchen soap and sponges by the sink—oh, and cake, too!

Linens & Baskets

♡ Give yourself towels you love—you are worth it, my love! They serve as covers for what just came out of the oven and to cozy the counter up and for everything else you need a linen for—gather the ones that feel good to you and look good, too

♡ Baskets of all sizes to hold, support, and gather everything you need

Machinery

♡ Stainless steel or copper kettle

♡ Rice cooker

♡ Slow cooker (ceramic base, glass top)

♡ Cuisinart (food processor!)

♡ Vitamix

♡ Stand mixer

♡ Hand mixer

♡ Immersion blender

♡ Juicer

♡ Air fryer (LOVE)

Time to Let Go of . . .

Anything that doesn't say YES to you must go now!

All plastic things that cause all kind of cray things in the body.

The white or any plastic poultry cutting boards, thin or thick.

Towels that feel like they are rags or for the bathroom.

Those huge ladles and spoons that are for catering jobs (unless you need them for catering jobs—then they can go in the catering area).

All the black plastic spoons or anything plastic that goes on heat or in the freezer.

Anything stained, coated, or nonstick—these items can be sticky for your health.

Here is the permission to finally let that stuff go!

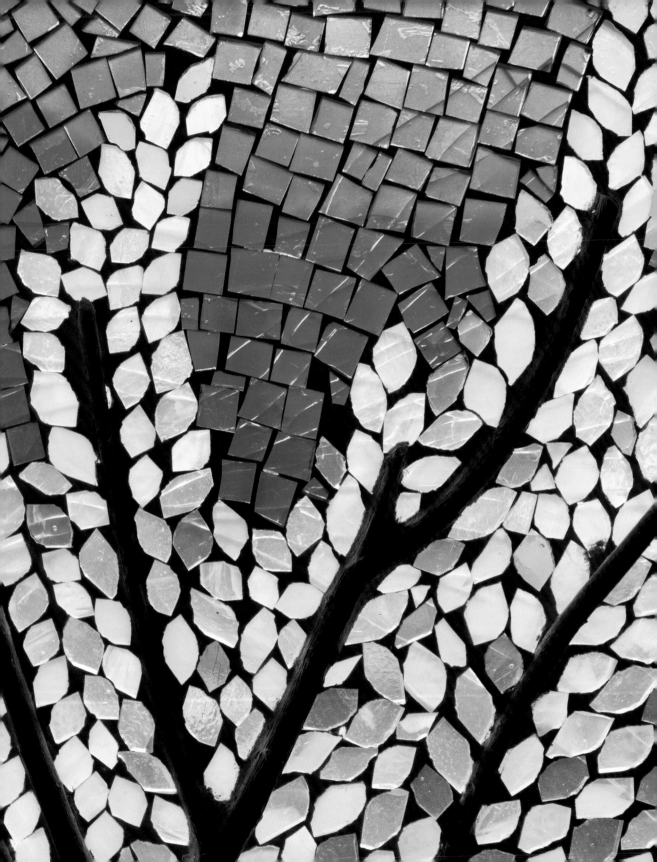

POEMS THAT HEAL

Poetry is the bridge. It is a forever healer. Here, I offer you a few of the poems that have found me at different times in my life and that continue to awaken something inside of me. They softened, shaped, and formed who I am today. They are mothers, fathers, shamans, elders; they are word tinctures that make their way into the crevices of our lives. They mend us back together. As you go on a journey to seek, find, and excavate these poems, lean into the words. Get closer to the unknown inside the rhythm of a stanza. Read it aloud, then repeat it to yourself again and again until it dissolves into the earth that is you. Maybe you will emerge with wisdom you didn't have before. Go to the poem that calls you first. Then find the rest. Then find more of your own. I am so excited for you.

"Phenomenal Woman" by Maya Angelou

"The Thing Is" by Ellen Bass

"The Things That Scare You" by Hiro Boga

"Blessing the Boats" by Lucille Clifton

"The Lanyard" by Billy Collins

"The Size of the Love Bruise" by Hafiz

"The Sun in Drag" by Hafiz

"Eagle Poem" by Joy Harjo

"Perhaps the World Ends Here" by Joy Harjo

"Inside" by Linda Hogan

"To Be Held" by Linda Hogan

"When the Body" by Linda Hogan

"Hurry" by Marie Howe

"Thanks" by W. S. Merwin

"The Quiet Power" by Tara Mohr

"In Love with the World" by Mark Nepo

"Famous" by Naomi Shihab Nye

"Kindness" by Naomi Shihab Nye

"Voices" by Naomi Shihab Nye

"For Courage" by John O'Donohue

"First Hour" by Sharon Olds

"Flare" by Mary Oliver

"I Go Down to the Shore" by Mary Oliver

"Praying" by Mary Oliver

"Thirst" by Mary Oliver

"The Love Cook" by Ron Padgett

"The Waiting Place" by Dr. Seuss

"The Loser" by Shel Silverstein

"Good Bones" by Maggie Smith

"Love After Love" by Derek Walcott

"Everything Is Waiting for You" by David Whyte

"The House of Belonging" by David Whyte

"Just Beyond Yourself" by David Whyte

BOOKS THAT HOLD

The books that follow have been my teachers, guides, mentors, and healers. They have gathered around me in the most challenging of times, extending their word-filled arms, carrying me from one place to another, as I journeyed toward myself. I have read from these to groups, retreats, sessions, and more. The healing in these books ripple out far and wide. These writers are pioneers, paving the path for us to be here together. I am forever grateful for their healing journeys. Create a special place for your library. Take your time with each book. Show up to these words and let them land where you need them. They will carry you as far as you need to go. Then the next one will show up to take you a little further along. You can always begin again. You just have to start with one.

Life-Changers by the Altar

The Courage to Change—One Day at a Time by Al-Anon Family Groups

Living Beautifully with Uncertainty and Change by Pema Chödrön

Co-Dependents Anonymous by Coda Conference Literature

Beauty and the Soul: The Extraordinary Power of Everyday Beauty to Heal Your Life by Piero Ferrucci

Notes on the Need for Beauty by J. Ruth Gendler

No Mud, No Lotus: The Art of Transforming Suffering by Thich Nhat Hanh

The Book of Medicines by Linda Hogan

I Ching: The Symbolic Life by Stephen Karcher, PhD

Tao Te Ching (a new English version) by Stephen Mitchell

The Book of Awakening by Mark Nepo

Finding Inner Courage by Mark Nepo

Things That Join the Sea and the Sky: Field Notes on Living by Mark Nepo

Anam Cara by John O'Donohue

Beauty: The Invisible Embrace by John O'Donohue

Bless the Space Between Us: A Book of Blessings by John O'Donohue

Devotions: The Selected Poems of Mary Oliver

Kitchen Table Wisdom: Stories That Heal by Rachel Naomi Remen, MD

Sweat Your Prayers: Movement as Spiritual Practice by Gabrielle Roth

The Wildwood Tarot: Wherein Wisdom Resides by Mark Ryan and John Matthews

Parenting from the Inside Out: How a Deeper Self-Understanding Can Help You Raise Children Who Thrive by Daniel J. Siegel and Mary Hartzell

Wild Mercy: Living the Fierce and Tender Wisdom of the Women Mystics by Mirabai Starr

Nejma by Nayyirah Waheed

salt. by Nayyirah Waheed

Healing Your Creativity Story

Art & Fear: Observations on the Perils (and Rewards) of Artmaking by David Bayles and Ted Orland

Braving the Wilderness: The Quest for True Belonging by Brené Brown

Big Magic: Creative Living Beyond Fear by Elizabeth Gilbert

The War of Art: Break Through the Blocks and Win Your Inner Creative Battles by Steven Pressfield

You Are a Badass: How to Stop Doubting Your Greatness and Start Living an Awesome Life by Jen Sincero

Rewriting Your Money Story

Time Warrior: How to Defeat Procrastination, People-Pleasing, Self-Doubt, Over-Commitment, Broken Promises and Chaos by Steve Chandler

Wealth Warrior: The Personal Prosperity Revolution by Steve Chandler

The Prosperous Coach: Increase Income and Impact for You and Your Clients by Steve Chandler and Rich Litvin

You Are a Badass at Making Money: Master the Mindset of Wealth by Jen Sincero

Overcoming Underearning: A Simple Guide to a Richer Life by Barbara Stanny

Sacred Success: A Course in Financial Miracles by Barbara Stanny

Waiting for Me to Read

No Cure for Being Human (And Other Truths I Need to Hear) by Kate Bowler

Native Science: Natural Laws of Interdependence by Gregory Cajete

I Have Been Assigned the Single Bird: A Daughter's Memoir by Susan Cerulean

Complete Poems by E. E. Cummings

Being a Human: Adventures in Forty Thousand Years of Consciousness by Charles Foster

Finding Freedom: A Cook's Story by Erin French

Poet Warrior: A Memoir by Joy Harjo

The Book of Longings by Sue Monk Kidd

Braiding Sweetgrass by Robin Wall Kimmerer

Shikasta by Doris Lessing

Horizon by Barry Lopez

My Grandmother's Hands: Racialized Trauma and the Pathway to Mending Our Hearts and Bodies by Resmaa Menakem

Entering the Ghost River: Meditations on the Theory and Practice of Healing by Deena Metzger

How I Became a Tree: Discovering the Wisdom of the Forest by Sumana Roy

Finding the Mother Tree by Suzanne Simard

Kick-Ass Pioneers on Repeat

Zach Bush, MD

Pema Chödrön

Ram Dass

Larry Dossey

Donna Eden

The Gottman Institute

Stephen Karcher, PhD

Eileen Kenny, DC

Peter A. Levine, PhD

Gabor Maté, MD

Deena Metzger

Michael Pollan

Rachel Naomi Remen, MD

Krista Tippet and the *On Being* podcast

SAND: Science and Nonduality

Anthony William

Just to get you started . . .

Cookbooks to Keep Close By

An Everlasting Meal: Cooking with Economy and Grace by Tamar Adler

The Great Dixter Cookbook: Recipes from an English Garden by Aaron Bertelsen

A Twist of the Wrist by Carolyn Carreño and Nancy Silverton

Apples for Jam: Recipes for Life and all books by Tessa Kiros

Baked: New Frontiers in Flavor by Matt Lewis and Renato Poliafito

Jamie at Home: Cook Your Way to the Good Life by Jamie Oliver

Savor: Rustic Recipes Inspired by Forest, Field, and Farm by Ilona Oppenheim

Healing with Whole Foods: Asian Traditions and Modern Nutrition by Paul Pitchford

The Violet Bakery Cookbook by Claire Ptak

My Kitchen Year: 136 Recipes That Saved My Life by Ruth Reichl

The Joy of Cooking by Irma S. Rombauer and Marion Rombauer Becker

Ripe, Tender, Notes from the Larder, Eat and all books by Nigel Slater

Eat Drink Live: 150 Recipes for Every Time of Day by Fran Warde

NOTES

1. Oxford Languages, s.v. "Permission," languages.oup.com/google-dictionary -en/ (accessed March 2021).

2. Oxford Languages, s.v. "Nourish," languages.oup.com/google-dictionary-en/ (accessed March 2021).

3. Oxford Languages, s.v. "Become," languages.oup.com/google-dictionary-en/ (accessed March 2021).

4. Pema Chödrön, *The Pocket Pema Chödrön*, ed. Eden Steinberg (Boston: Shambala Publications, 2008).

5. Mark Nepo, *The Book of Awakening* (Newburyport, MA: Conari Press, 2011).

6. Oxford Languages, s.v. "Angst," languages.oup.com/google-dictionary-en/ (accessed March 2021).

7. Mark Nepo, *The Book of Awakening*.

8. Oxford Languages, s.v. "Tending," languages.oup.com/google-dictionary-en/ (accessed March 2021).

9. Gabrielle Roth, *Sweat Your Prayers: Movement as Spiritual Practice* (New York: Penguin Putnam, 1997).

10. Gabrielle Roth, *Sweat Your Prayers*.

11. Gabrielle Roth, *Sweat Your Prayers*.

12. Gabrielle Roth, *Sweat Your Prayers*.

13. David Whyte, *The Bell and The Blackbird* (Vancouver, BC: Many Rivers Press, 2018). Used with permission.

14. Tamar Adler, *An Everlasting Meal: Cooking With Economy and Grace* (New York: Scribner, 2011).

15. E. E. Cummings, "Love is a Place," *Complete Poems 1904–1962*, ed. George James Firmage (© 1935, 1963, 1991 by the Trustees for the E. E. Cummings Trust). Copyright © 1978 by George James Firmage.

16. Oxford Languages, s.v. "To Be," languages.oup.com/google-dictionary-en/ (accessed June 2021).

17. Oxford Languages, s.v. "Being," languages.oup.com/google-dictionary-en/ (accessed June 2021).

18. Oxford Languages, s.v. "Banshee," languages.oup.com/google-dictionary-en/ (accessed August 2021).

19. J. Ruth Gendler, *The Book of Qualities* (New York: William Morrow, 1984).

20. John O'Donohue, "Becoming Wise," interview by Krista Tippet, *The On Being Project*, March 18, 2016. Used with permission.

21. Piero Ferrucci, *Beauty and the Soul: The Extraordinary Power of Everyday Beauty to Heal Your Life*, trans. Vivien Reid Ferrucci (New York: Penguin, 2009).

22. Oxford Languages, s.v. "Rhythm," languages.oup.com/google-dictionary-en/ (accessed March 2021).

23. Oxford Languages, s.v. "Tending," languages.oup.com/google-dictionary-en/ (accessed March 2021).

24. Steven Mintz, "What are Values?" *Ethics Sage* (blog), August 8, 2018, ethicssage.com/2018/08/what-are-values.html.

25. John O'Donohue, *Anam Cara: A Book of Celtic Wisdom* (New York: Harper Collins, 1997).

26. John O'Donohue, "Becoming Wise."

27. Ralph Waldo Emerson, *Self-Reliance and Other Essays* (Mineola, NY: Dover Publications, 1993).

28. Mary Oliver, "Messenger," *Thirst*, (Boston: Beacon Press, 2006).

29. Oxford Languages, s.v. "Healing," languages.oup.com/google-dictionary-en/ (accessed August 2021).

ABOUT THE AUTHOR

Jules Blaine Davis, the Kitchen Healer, is a devoted mother, artist, poet, and pioneer in the field of healing as a living. She is a way-shower to nourishing our deepest lives. Over the last fifteen years in private practice, leading retreats and gathering circles of women around the fire and kitchen island, Jules has discovered a lineage of longing we carry in our bodies. She is an activist for this longing, and the hunger that comes with it. She has found that these callings in us are the essential ingredients to meeting our deeper selves. Jules is a holder for our stories, our bodies, our day-to-day rhythms as she shines the headlamp or freedom torch on the wisdom in our becoming. She invites us to awaken inside this life, transforming it into a life we love, in and out of the kitchen. Jules lives with her family in Los Angeles, California.

ABOUT SOUNDS TRUE

Sounds True is a multimedia publisher whose mission is to inspire and support personal transformation and spiritual awakening. Founded in 1985 and located in Boulder, Colorado, we work with many of the leading spiritual teachers, thinkers, healers, and visionary artists of our time. We strive with every title to preserve the essential "living wisdom" of the author or artist. It is our goal to create products that not only provide information to a reader or listener but also embody the quality of a wisdom transmission.

For those seeking genuine transformation, Sounds True is your trusted partner. At SoundsTrue.com you will find a wealth of free resources to support your journey, including exclusive weekly audio interviews, free downloads, interactive learning tools, and other special savings on all our titles.

To learn more, please visit SoundsTrue.com/freegifts or call us toll-free at 800.333.9185.

sounds true
WAKING UP THE WORLD